PfMP Exam Companion

Q&A with Explanations

SUJAN MUKHERJEE

CONTENTS

Introduction

Welcome to the "PfMP Exam Companion: Q&A with Explanations" – your comprehensive guide to preparing for the Portfolio Management Professional (PfMP) exam. This book is designed to help you master the intricate world of portfolio management and succeed in obtaining your PfMP certification. Whether you're an experienced portfolio manager or aspiring to enhance your skills, this book is tailored to provide you with a deep understanding of the PfMP exam content.

Why This Book:

Navigating the complexities of portfolio management requires not only knowledge but also the ability to apply that knowledge effectively. This book goes beyond mere rote learning by offering a collection of challenging questions and detailed explanations. Each question is carefully crafted to mirror the diversity and depth of the PfMP exam. The comprehensive explanations break down the answers, providing insights into the rationale and concepts behind each correct choice and helping you grasp the intricacies of portfolio management principles.

Key Features:

Diverse Question Bank: Explore a wide range of questions that cover every domain and aspect of portfolio management, ensuring thorough preparation for the exam.

Detailed Explanations: Gain in-depth insights into each question's correct answer and understand the underlying concepts, aiding your comprehension and retention.

Real-world Scenarios: Experience scenarios that mirror real-life portfolio management situations, enhancing your ability to apply theoretical knowledge to practical scenarios.

Comprehensive Coverage: Cover all five PfMP domains, including Strategic Alignment, Governance, Portfolio Performance, Portfolio Risk Management, and Communications Management.

Your PfMP Success Path:

As you embark on your PfMP journey, this book serves as your trusted companion. Use it as an instrument to assess your understanding, reinforce your knowledge, and develop the critical thinking skills required to excel in the PfMP exam. Prepare with confidence and be ready to showcase your expertise in portfolio management. Good luck on your journey to becoming a certified Portfolio Management Professional!

PRACTICE TEST - 1

Question 1:

Which of the following is NOT a key function of portfolio management?

A) Resource allocation

B) Risk management

C) Agile development

D) Strategic alignment

Answer: C) Agile development

Explanation: Portfolio management focuses on strategic alignment, resource allocation, and risk management to ensure projects and programs contribute to the organization's goals. While agile principles are essential in project and program management, they are not a core function of portfolio management.

Question 2:

What is the primary purpose of a portfolio charter in portfolio management?

A) Define project deliverables

B) Identify stakeholder expectations

C) Establish governance structure

D) Describe the financial benefits

Answer: C) Establish governance structure

Explanation: The portfolio charter defines the governance structure, roles, responsibilities, and decision-making authority for managing the portfolio. It provides a clear framework for ensuring alignment and effective decision-making across the portfolio components.

Question 3:

In portfolio management, which term refers to the amount of value an organization can expect to gain from its portfolio investments over a specific time period?

A) Portfolio value

B) ROI projection

C) Portfolio yield

D) Value realization

Answer: A) Portfolio value

Explanation: Portfolio value represents the total expected value an organization anticipates from its portfolio investments, considering factors like financial returns, strategic benefits, and risk management.

Question 4:

What is the purpose of a strategic roadmap in portfolio management?

A) To outline project schedules

B) To prioritize portfolio components

C) To visualize resource allocation

D) To communicate strategic objectives

Answer: D) To communicate strategic objectives

Explanation: A strategic roadmap visually communicates the organization's strategic objectives and initiatives to stakeholders. It provides a clear overview of the portfolio's direction and priorities, fostering alignment and understanding.

Question 5:

Which portfolio management process involves assessing and adjusting portfolio components based on performance and changing circumstances?

A) Portfolio optimization

B) Portfolio monitoring and reporting

C) Portfolio governance

D) Portfolio initiation

Answer: B) Portfolio monitoring and reporting

Explanation: Portfolio monitoring and reporting involve tracking the performance of portfolio components, identifying variances, and making necessary adjustments to ensure alignment with strategic goals.

Question 6:

Which type of portfolio management office (PMO) focuses on providing support, training, and tools for portfolio management across the organization?

A) Directive PMO

B) Controlling PMO

C) Supportive PMO

D) Delivery PMO

Answer: C) Supportive PMO

Explanation: A supportive PMO assists in providing tools, training, and best practices for portfolio management to ensure consistency and improve portfolio performance.

Question 7:

What is the main purpose of the portfolio risk management process in portfolio management?

A) To eliminate all project risks

B) To identify and mitigate risks across the portfolio

C) To outsource risk management to external consultants

D) To allocate risk to individual projects

Answer: B) To identify and mitigate risks across the portfolio

Explanation: The portfolio risk management process involves identifying, assessing, and mitigating risks that could impact the achievement of portfolio objectives. It ensures that risks are managed at a strategic level to minimize negative impacts.

Question 8:

Which stage of the portfolio management lifecycle involves selecting and prioritizing potential portfolio components for inclusion?

A) Initiation

B) Planning

C) Execution

D) Closing

Answer: B) Planning

Explanation: The planning stage of the portfolio management lifecycle involves evaluating potential portfolio components, selecting the most beneficial ones, and prioritizing them based on strategic goals and resource constraints.

Question 9:

What is the primary purpose of a portfolio management framework in portfolio management?

A) To provide project management templates

B) To establish a standardized project lifecycle

C) To define governance and decision-making processes

D) To track financial performance

Answer: C) To define governance and decision-making processes

Explanation: A portfolio management framework outlines the governance structure, roles, responsibilities, and decision-making processes for managing the portfolio components to ensure strategic alignment and effective management.

Question 10:

What is a key benefit of conducting regular portfolio reviews in portfolio management?

A) Reducing project risks

B) Increasing stakeholder satisfaction

C) Ensuring compliance with regulations

D) Identifying underperforming components

Answer: D) Identifying underperforming components

Explanation: Regular portfolio reviews help identify underperforming components early, allowing for corrective actions and resource reallocation to ensure the portfolio remains aligned with strategic goals.

Question 11:

Which component of the PfMP® domain framework involves the allocation of resources to portfolio components?

A) Portfolio governance

B) Portfolio risk management

C) Portfolio value management

D) Portfolio communication management

Answer: C) Portfolio value management

Explanation: Portfolio value management includes resource allocation to ensure that the portfolio components generate the maximum value for the organization.

Question 12:

In portfolio management, what is the purpose of a portfolio component register?

A) To track financial expenditures

B) To manage project schedules

C) To store project artifacts

D) To capture and organize component information

Answer: D) To capture and organize component information

Explanation: The portfolio component register captures and organizes information about the components included in the portfolio, including their objectives, benefits, risks, and alignment with strategic goals.

Question 13:

Which of the following is a key consideration in the portfolio governance process in portfolio management?

A) Scheduling project tasks

B) Calculating earned value

C) Prioritizing components

D) Defining work breakdown structures

Answer: C) Prioritizing components

Explanation: Portfolio governance involves the process of prioritizing and allocating resources to portfolio components based on their alignment with strategic goals and expected value.

Question 14:

What is the primary goal of a portfolio management office (PMO) in portfolio management?

A) To manage individual projects

B) To provide financial reporting

C) To ensure compliance with regulations

D) To support the execution of the portfolio strategy

Answer: D) To support the execution of the portfolio strategy

Explanation: The primary goal of a portfolio management office (PMO) is to support the execution of the organization's portfolio strategy by providing guidance, oversight, and governance.

Question 15:

Which of the following statements accurately describes portfolio management in an organizational context?

A) Portfolio management focuses only on individual projects

B) Portfolio management ensures that project managers have sufficient resources

C) Portfolio management is concerned with the alignment and prioritization of projects and programs

D) Portfolio management is primarily responsible for project execution

Answer: C) Portfolio management is concerned with the alignment and prioritization of projects and programs

Explanation: Portfolio management ensures that the organization's projects and programs are aligned with its strategic goals and prioritized for optimal resource allocation and value generation.

Question 16:

In portfolio management, what is the primary purpose of conducting a benefit realization review?

A) To evaluate project performance

B) To identify risks and issues

C) To assess strategic alignment

D) To measure the achievement of benefits

Answer: D) To measure the achievement of benefits

Explanation: A benefit realization review assesses whether the expected benefits of portfolio components have been achieved and whether they contribute to the organization's strategic goals.

Question 17:

Which of the following is a key role in portfolio management responsible for facilitating the execution of the portfolio strategy?

A) Project manager

B) Portfolio manager

C) Business analyst

D) Change manager

Answer: B) Portfolio manager

Explanation: The portfolio manager is responsible for facilitating the execution of the portfolio strategy by aligning and prioritizing projects and programs to maximize value and achieve strategic objectives.

Question 18:

What is the primary purpose of conducting portfolio reviews in portfolio management?

A) To evaluate individual project performance

B) To assess the performance of the portfolio as a whole

C) To allocate resources to portfolio components

D) To track project schedules

Answer: B) To assess the performance of the portfolio as a whole

Explanation: Portfolio reviews assess the overall performance of the portfolio, including the alignment of components with strategic goals and the allocation of resources to achieve the desired outcomes.

Question 19:

Which type of portfolio management involves evaluating potential portfolio components based on their financial return on investment (ROI)?

A) Strategic portfolio management

B) Financial portfolio management

C) Resource portfolio management

D) Value-based portfolio management

Answer: B) Financial portfolio management

Explanation: Financial portfolio management involves evaluating potential components based on their financial return on investment (ROI) to ensure the optimal allocation of resources.

Question 20:

What is the primary objective of portfolio management reporting in portfolio management?

A) To track project tasks

B) To calculate earned value

C) To assess stakeholder satisfaction

D) To provide visibility into portfolio performance

Answer: D) To provide visibility into portfolio performance

Explanation: Portfolio management reporting provides stakeholders with visibility into the performance of the portfolio, including progress, risks, and alignment with strategic goals.

Question 21:

Which component of portfolio management involves evaluating portfolio components based on their alignment with the organization's strategic objectives?

A) Portfolio governance

B) Portfolio risk management

C) Portfolio value management

D) Portfolio communication management

Answer: C) Portfolio value management

Explanation: Portfolio value management involves assessing portfolio components to ensure their alignment with the organization's strategic objectives and value generation.

Question 22:

What is the primary purpose of a portfolio roadmap in portfolio management?

A) To define project schedules

B) To allocate resources

C) To communicate strategic priorities

D) To track financial performance

Answer: C) To communicate strategic priorities

Explanation: A portfolio roadmap communicates the organization's strategic priorities and initiatives to stakeholders, providing a visual representation of the planned sequence of projects and programs.

Question 23:

In portfolio management, what is the main goal of portfolio optimization?

A) To eliminate project risks

B) To maximize the number of projects

C) To achieve the highest portfolio value

D) To ensure equal resource allocation

Answer: C) To achieve the highest portfolio value

Explanation: Portfolio optimization aims to select and prioritize portfolio components in a way that maximizes the overall portfolio value and aligns with the organization's strategic objectives.

Question 24:

What is the primary role of a portfolio steering committee in portfolio management?

A) To manage individual projects

B) To allocate project resources

C) To provide guidance and oversight

D) To execute project tasks

Answer: C) To provide guidance and oversight

Explanation: A portfolio steering committee provides guidance, oversight, and decision-making authority to ensure that portfolio components align with strategic goals and are effectively managed.

Question 25:

Which type of portfolio management focuses on optimizing the organization's portfolio based on cost, risk, and resource constraints?

A) Strategic portfolio management

B) Financial portfolio management

C) Resource portfolio management

D) Value-based portfolio management

Answer: B) Financial portfolio management

Explanation: Financial portfolio management optimizes the portfolio based on cost, risk, and resource constraints to ensure efficient allocation of resources and value generation.

Question 26:

What is the primary purpose of a benefits dependency network in portfolio management?

A) To track project schedules

B) To calculate earned value

C) To visualize project relationships

D) To allocate project resources

Answer: C) To visualize project relationships

Explanation: A benefits dependency network visualizes the relationships between portfolio components, helping stakeholders understand how components depend on each other to achieve desired outcomes.

Question 27:

In portfolio management, what is the purpose of a portfolio risk register?

A) To track project expenditures

B) To manage project schedules

C) To store project artifacts

D) To capture and manage risks

Answer: D) To capture and manage risks

Explanation: A portfolio risk register captures and manages risks associated with portfolio components, enabling proactive risk management to ensure strategic alignment and value realization.

Question 28:

What is the main goal of portfolio governance in portfolio management?

A) To execute project tasks

B) To allocate project resources

C) To ensure compliance with regulations

D) To align portfolio components with strategic goals

Answer: D) To align portfolio components with strategic goals

Explanation: Portfolio governance ensures that portfolio components align with strategic goals, prioritize resource allocation, and contribute to the organization's overall success.

Question 29:

Which component of the PfMP® domain framework involves ensuring that portfolio components are aligned with the organization's strategic objectives?

A) Portfolio governance

B) Portfolio risk management

C) Portfolio value management

D) Portfolio communication management

Answer: C) Portfolio value management

Explanation: Portfolio value management involves ensuring that portfolio components align with the organization's strategic objectives to maximize value generation.

Question 30:

In portfolio management, what is the purpose of a portfolio benefits realization plan?

A) To track project schedules

B) To allocate project resources

C) To calculate earned value

D) To ensure benefits are achieved

Answer: D) To ensure benefits are achieved

Explanation: A portfolio benefits realization plan outlines the approach for tracking, measuring, and ensuring the achievement of expected benefits from portfolio components.

Question 31:

Which stage of the portfolio management lifecycle involves evaluating and selecting potential portfolio components for inclusion?

A) Initiation

B) Planning

C) Execution

D) Closing

Answer: B) Planning

Explanation: The planning stage of the portfolio management lifecycle involves evaluating potential portfolio components, selecting the most beneficial ones, and prioritizing them based on strategic goals and resource constraints.

Question 32:

What is the primary purpose of portfolio management reporting in portfolio management?

A) To track project tasks

B) To assess stakeholder satisfaction

C) To calculate earned value

D) To provide visibility into portfolio performance

Answer: D) To provide visibility into portfolio performance

Explanation: Portfolio management reporting provides stakeholders with visibility into the performance of the portfolio, including progress, risks, and alignment with strategic goals.

Question 33:

Which role in portfolio management is responsible for ensuring that the portfolio components are aligned with the organization's strategic goals?

A) Project manager

B) Portfolio manager

C) Business analyst

D) Change manager

Answer: B) Portfolio manager

Explanation: The portfolio manager is responsible for ensuring that portfolio components are aligned with the organization's strategic goals and priorities, maximizing value generation.

Question 34:

What is the main objective of conducting a portfolio review in portfolio management?

A) To assess the performance of individual projects

B) To allocate resources to portfolio components

C) To track project schedules

D) To evaluate the overall portfolio performance

Answer: D) To evaluate the overall portfolio performance

Explanation: A portfolio review evaluates the performance of the overall portfolio, assessing its alignment with strategic goals, resource allocation, and value delivery.

Question 35:

In portfolio management, which type of portfolio management focuses on selecting and prioritizing portfolio components based on their strategic alignment and expected value?

A) Strategic portfolio management

B) Financial portfolio management

C) Resource portfolio management

D) Value-based portfolio management

Answer: A) Strategic portfolio management

Explanation: Strategic portfolio management focuses on selecting and prioritizing portfolio components that align with the organization's strategic goals and maximize value delivery.

Question 36:

What is the primary goal of conducting a portfolio component review in portfolio management?

A) To track project tasks

B) To evaluate individual project performance

C) To calculate earned value

D) To assess stakeholder satisfaction

Answer: B) To evaluate individual project performance

Explanation: A portfolio component review evaluates the performance of individual projects or programs within the portfolio, assessing their progress and contribution to strategic goals.

Question 37:

In portfolio management, what is the purpose of a portfolio management plan?

A) To track project schedules

B) To allocate project resources

C) To calculate earned value

D) To guide portfolio management activities

Answer: D) To guide portfolio management activities

Explanation: A portfolio management plan outlines the approach, processes, and guidelines for managing the portfolio, ensuring alignment with strategic objectives and value generation.

Question 38:

Which type of portfolio management involves evaluating potential portfolio components based on their financial feasibility and return on investment (ROI)?

A) Strategic portfolio management

B) Financial portfolio management

C) Resource portfolio management

D) Value-based portfolio management

Answer: B) Financial portfolio management

Explanation: Financial portfolio management involves evaluating potential portfolio components based on financial feasibility, ROI, and resource allocation to achieve the organization's strategic goals.

Question 39:

What is the primary goal of portfolio communication management in portfolio management?

A) To track project tasks

B) To allocate project resources

C) To ensure compliance with regulations

D) To provide effective communication to stakeholders

Answer: D) To provide effective communication to stakeholders

Explanation: Portfolio communication management focuses on delivering relevant and timely information to stakeholders, ensuring clear communication about portfolio components, progress, and alignment with strategic goals.

Question 40:

In portfolio management, which type of portfolio management focuses on optimizing resource allocation to ensure the successful execution of portfolio components?

A) Strategic portfolio management

B) Financial portfolio management

C) Resource portfolio management

D) Value-based portfolio management

Answer: C) Resource portfolio management

Explanation: Resource portfolio management optimizes the allocation of resources to ensure the successful execution of portfolio components while considering constraints and strategic priorities.

Question 41:

What is the main purpose of a portfolio management office (PMO) in portfolio management?

A) To execute project tasks

B) To allocate project resources

C) To provide project templates

D) To provide governance and oversight

Answer: D) To provide governance and oversight

Explanation: A portfolio management office (PMO) provides governance, oversight, and guidance to ensure that portfolio components align with strategic goals and adhere to established standards.

Question 42:

Which portfolio management component involves identifying and managing interdependencies between portfolio components?

A) Portfolio governance

B) Portfolio risk management

C) Portfolio value management

D) Portfolio communication management

Answer: D) Portfolio communication management

Explanation: Portfolio communication management involves identifying and managing interdependencies between portfolio components to ensure effective coordination and alignment with strategic goals.

Question 43:

What is the primary goal of portfolio financial management in portfolio management?

A) To track project schedules

B) To allocate project resources

C) To ensure compliance with regulations

D) To optimize financial resources for portfolio components

Answer: D) To optimize financial resources for portfolio components

Explanation: Portfolio financial management aims to optimize the allocation of financial resources to portfolio components to achieve strategic goals while adhering to financial constraints.

Question 44:

In portfolio management, which stage involves reviewing and approving the portfolio components for execution?

A) Initiation

B) Planning

C) Execution

D) Monitoring and controlling

Answer: B) Planning

Explanation: During the planning stage, portfolio components are reviewed and approved for execution based on their alignment with strategic goals and available resources.

Question 45:

Which type of portfolio management focuses on managing the allocation of resources across portfolio components to achieve optimal results?

A) Strategic portfolio management

B) Financial portfolio management

C) Resource portfolio management

D) Value-based portfolio management

Answer: C) Resource portfolio management

Explanation: Resource portfolio management focuses on managing the allocation of resources across portfolio components to achieve optimal results and alignment with strategic goals.

Question 46:

What is the main purpose of a portfolio dashboard in portfolio management?

A) To track project tasks

B) To calculate earned value

C) To provide visibility into portfolio performance

D) To allocate project resources

Answer: C) To provide visibility into portfolio performance

Explanation: A portfolio dashboard provides stakeholders with visualized data to understand the performance and status of the portfolio, including progress, risks, and alignment with strategic goals.

Question 47:

Which PfMP domain focuses on evaluating the organization's capacity and capability to execute portfolio components successfully?

A) Strategic alignment

B) Governance

C) Portfolio performance

D) Risk management

Answer: A) Strategic alignment

Explanation: The strategic alignment domain assesses the organization's capacity and capability to execute portfolio components successfully while ensuring alignment with strategic goals.

Question 48:

In portfolio management, what is the main objective of a portfolio benefit map?

A) To track project schedules

B) To allocate project resources

C) To visualize benefits realization

D) To assess stakeholder satisfaction

Answer: C) To visualize benefits realization

Explanation: A portfolio benefit map visually represents the planned benefits and their realization over time, helping stakeholders understand how benefits will be achieved through portfolio components.

Question 49:

What is the primary purpose of portfolio risk management in portfolio management?

A) To execute project tasks

B) To allocate project resources

C) To track project schedules

D) To identify, assess, and mitigate risks

Answer: D) To identify, assess, and mitigate risks

Explanation: Portfolio risk management involves identifying, assessing, and mitigating risks associated with portfolio components to ensure their successful execution and alignment with strategic goals.

Question 50:

Which portfolio management component involves evaluating the value and benefits generated by portfolio components?

A) Portfolio governance

B) Portfolio risk management

C) Portfolio value management

D) Portfolio communication management

Answer: C) Portfolio value management

Explanation: Portfolio value management involves evaluating the value and benefits generated by portfolio components to ensure alignment with strategic goals and value delivery.

Question 51:

In portfolio management, what is the main goal of a portfolio prioritization matrix?

A) To allocate project resources

B) To track project schedules

C) To calculate earned value

D) To prioritize and rank portfolio components

Answer: D) To prioritize and rank portfolio components

Explanation: A portfolio prioritization matrix helps prioritize and rank portfolio components based on predefined criteria, enabling the organization to make informed decisions about resource allocation and execution.

Question 52:

Which role in portfolio management is responsible for overseeing the entire portfolio and ensuring its alignment with strategic goals?

A) Project manager

B) Portfolio manager

C) Program manager

D) Business analyst

Answer: B) Portfolio manager

Explanation: The portfolio manager oversees the entire portfolio, ensuring its alignment with strategic goals, managing resources, and maximizing value generation.

Question 53:

What is the primary purpose of portfolio benefits realization in portfolio management?

A) To allocate project resources

B) To track project schedules

C) To ensure that the expected benefits are achieved

D) To identify and assess risks

Answer: C) To ensure that the expected benefits are achieved

Explanation: Portfolio benefits realization focuses on ensuring that the expected benefits from portfolio components are achieved and contribute to the organization's strategic goals.

Question 54:

Which PfMP domain involves defining the organization's strategic goals and objectives that drive portfolio components' selection and execution?

A) Strategic alignment

B) Governance

C) Portfolio performance

D) Risk management

Answer: A) Strategic alignment

Explanation: The strategic alignment domain involves defining the organization's strategic goals and objectives, which drive the selection and execution of portfolio components to achieve desired outcomes.

Question 55:

In portfolio management, what is the main goal of a portfolio review board?

A) To execute project tasks

B) To allocate project resources

C) To assess project schedules

D) To provide governance and oversight

Answer: D) To provide governance and oversight

Explanation: A portfolio review board provides governance and oversight to ensure that portfolio components align with strategic goals, adhere to standards, and maximize value generation.

Question 56:

Which type of portfolio management involves evaluating the financial performance and benefits realization of portfolio components?

A) Strategic portfolio management

B) Financial portfolio management

C) Resource portfolio management

D) Value-based portfolio management

Answer: B) Financial portfolio management

Explanation: Financial portfolio management involves evaluating the financial performance and benefits realization of portfolio components, ensuring alignment with strategic goals and financial objectives.

Question 57:

What is the main objective of conducting a portfolio assessment in portfolio management?

A) To allocate project resources

B) To track project schedules

C) To assess individual project performance

D) To evaluate the overall portfolio performance

Answer: D) To evaluate the overall portfolio performance

Explanation: A portfolio assessment evaluates the overall portfolio performance, including progress, risks, alignment with strategic goals, and value generation.

Question 58:

Which PfMP domain focuses on defining and implementing the governance structure and processes for managing the portfolio?

A) Strategic alignment

B) Governance

C) Portfolio performance

D) Risk management

Answer: B) Governance

Explanation: The governance domain focuses on defining and implementing the governance structure, processes, and guidelines for managing the portfolio, ensuring alignment with strategic goals and value delivery.

Question 59:

In portfolio management, what is the primary goal of a portfolio charter?

A) To track project schedules

B) To allocate project resources

C) To define the scope and objectives of the portfolio

D) To calculate earned value

Answer: C) To define the scope and objectives of the portfolio

Explanation: A portfolio charter defines the scope, objectives, and purpose of the portfolio, providing a clear understanding of the portfolio's goals and alignment with strategic objectives.

Question 60:

Which portfolio management component focuses on defining the roles, responsibilities, and authorities within the portfolio management framework?

A) Portfolio governance

B) Portfolio risk management

C) Portfolio value management

D) Portfolio communication management

Answer: A) Portfolio governance

Explanation: Portfolio governance focuses on defining the roles, responsibilities, and authorities within the portfolio management framework, ensuring effective decision-making, accountability, and alignment with strategic goals.

Question 61:

Which PfMP domain involves defining and implementing the processes and methodologies for managing the portfolio components?

A) Strategic alignment

B) Governance

C) Portfolio performance

D) Risk management

Answer: C) Portfolio performance

Explanation: The portfolio performance domain focuses on defining and implementing the processes, methodologies, and practices for managing the portfolio components effectively and efficiently.

Question 62:

In portfolio management, what is the main objective of a portfolio roadmap?

A) To allocate project resources

B) To track project schedules

C) To visualize the timeline and sequencing of portfolio components

D) To calculate earned value

Answer: C) To visualize the timeline and sequencing of portfolio components

Explanation: A portfolio roadmap visually represents the timeline and sequencing of portfolio components, enabling stakeholders to understand the planned execution and dependencies.

Question 63:

Which role in portfolio management is responsible for ensuring that portfolio components adhere to established standards and guidelines?

A) Project manager

B) Portfolio manager

C) Program manager

D) Governance manager

Answer: D) Governance manager

Explanation: The governance manager is responsible for ensuring that portfolio components adhere to established standards, guidelines, and governance processes to ensure alignment with strategic goals.

Question 64:

What is the primary goal of portfolio resource management in portfolio management?

A) To execute project tasks

B) To allocate project resources

C) To calculate earned value

D) To assess individual project performance

Answer: B) To allocate project resources

Explanation: Portfolio resource management involves allocating project resources effectively to portfolio components to optimize performance, alignment with goals, and value generation.

Question 65:

Which type of portfolio management involves evaluating the organization's capacity and capability to execute portfolio components successfully?

A) Strategic portfolio management

B) Financial portfolio management

C) Resource portfolio management

D) Value-based portfolio management

Answer: C) Resource portfolio management

Explanation: Resource portfolio management involves evaluating the organization's capacity and capability to execute portfolio components successfully, ensuring alignment with strategic goals.

Question 66:

In portfolio management, what is the main objective of a portfolio communication plan?

A) To track project schedules

B) To allocate project resources

C) To ensure effective communication among stakeholders

D) To calculate earned value

Answer: C) To ensure effective communication among stakeholders

Explanation: A portfolio communication plan ensures that effective communication takes place among stakeholders, facilitating understanding, alignment, and informed decision-making.

Question 67:

Which PfMP domain focuses on evaluating the benefits, risks, and financial considerations of portfolio components?

A) Strategic alignment

B) Governance

C) Portfolio performance

D) Risk management

Answer: D) Risk management

Explanation: The risk management domain focuses on evaluating the benefits, risks, and financial considerations of portfolio components to ensure successful execution and alignment with strategic goals.

Question 68:

What is the main purpose of conducting a portfolio audit in portfolio management?

A) To track project schedules

B) To allocate project resources

C) To assess individual project performance

D) To evaluate the effectiveness of portfolio management practices

Answer: D) To evaluate the effectiveness of portfolio management practices

Explanation: A portfolio audit evaluates the effectiveness of portfolio management practices, processes, and performance, identifying areas for improvement and enhancement.

Question 69:

In portfolio management, what is the primary goal of a portfolio dependency analysis?

A) To allocate project resources

B) To track project schedules

C) To identify and manage interdependencies between portfolio components

D) To calculate earned value

Answer: C) To identify and manage interdependencies between portfolio components

Explanation: A portfolio dependency analysis identifies and manages interdependencies between portfolio components to ensure effective coordination and alignment with strategic goals.

Question 70:

Which PfMP domain involves evaluating the performance of portfolio components and identifying areas for improvement?

A) Strategic alignment

B) Governance

C) Portfolio performance

D) Risk management

Answer: C) Portfolio performance

Explanation: The portfolio performance domain involves evaluating the performance of portfolio components, identifying areas for improvement, and enhancing the execution to achieve strategic goals.

Question 71:

What is the main goal of portfolio risk management in portfolio management?

A) To execute project tasks

B) To allocate project resources

C) To track project schedules

D) To identify, assess, and mitigate risks

Answer: D) To identify, assess, and mitigate risks

Explanation: Portfolio risk management involves identifying, assessing, and mitigating risks associated with portfolio components to ensure successful execution and alignment with strategic goals.

Question 72:

Which portfolio management component focuses on defining the roles, responsibilities, and authorities within the portfolio management framework?

A) Portfolio governance

B) Portfolio risk management

C) Portfolio value management

D) Portfolio communication management

Answer: A) Portfolio governance

Explanation: Portfolio governance focuses on defining the roles, responsibilities, and authorities within the portfolio management framework, ensuring effective decision-making, accountability, and alignment with strategic goals.

Question 73:

What is the primary objective of a portfolio assessment in portfolio management?

A) To allocate project resources

B) To track project schedules

C) To assess individual project performance

D) To evaluate the overall portfolio performance

Answer: D) To evaluate the overall portfolio performance

Explanation: A portfolio assessment evaluates the overall portfolio performance, including progress, risks, alignment with strategic goals, and value generation.

Question 74:

Which role in portfolio management is responsible for selecting, prioritizing, and optimizing the portfolio components?

A) Project manager

B) Portfolio manager

C) Program manager

D) Governance manager

Answer: B) Portfolio manager

Explanation: The portfolio manager is responsible for selecting, prioritizing, and optimizing the portfolio components to achieve strategic goals and value generation.

Question 75:

In portfolio management, what is the main purpose of a portfolio dashboard?

A) To track project schedules

B) To allocate project resources

C) To visualize the performance and status of portfolio components

D) To calculate earned value

Answer: C) To visualize the performance and status of portfolio components

Explanation: A portfolio dashboard provides a visual representation of the performance and status of portfolio components, enabling stakeholders to make informed decisions and track progress.

Question 76:

Which PfMP domain focuses on defining and implementing the processes for selecting, prioritizing, and authorizing portfolio components?

A) Strategic alignment

B) Governance

C) Portfolio performance

D) Risk management

Answer: A) Strategic alignment

Explanation: The strategic alignment domain focuses on defining and implementing the processes for selecting, prioritizing, and authorizing portfolio components to achieve strategic goals.

Question 77:

What is the primary goal of portfolio value management in portfolio management?

A) To execute project tasks

B) To allocate project resources

C) To calculate earned value

D) To maximize value generation from portfolio components

Answer: D) To maximize value generation from portfolio components

Explanation: Portfolio value management aims to maximize value generation from portfolio components by ensuring alignment with strategic goals and optimizing resource allocation.

Question 78:

Which type of portfolio management involves evaluating the financial performance and benefits realization of portfolio components?

A) Strategic portfolio management

B) Financial portfolio management

C) Resource portfolio management

D) Value-based portfolio management

Answer: B) Financial portfolio management

Explanation: Financial portfolio management involves evaluating the financial performance and benefits realization of portfolio components, ensuring alignment with strategic goals and financial objectives.

Question 79:

In portfolio management, what is the main purpose of a portfolio assessment framework?

A) To allocate project resources

B) To track project schedules

C) To assess individual project performance

D) To evaluate the overall portfolio performance

Answer: D) To evaluate the overall portfolio performance

Explanation: A portfolio assessment framework evaluates the overall portfolio performance, including progress, risks, alignment with strategic goals, and value generation.

Question 80:

Which PfMP domain focuses on defining and implementing the processes for identifying, assessing, and mitigating risks related to portfolio components?

A) Strategic alignment

B) Governance

C) Portfolio performance

D) Risk management

Answer: D) Risk management

Explanation: The risk management domain focuses on defining and implementing the processes for identifying, assessing, and mitigating risks related to portfolio components to ensure successful execution and alignment with strategic goals.

Question 81:

Which PfMP domain focuses on ensuring that portfolio components adhere to established governance processes and policies?

A) Portfolio performance

B) Governance

C) Risk management

D) Value management

Answer: B) Governance

Explanation: The governance domain in PfMP focuses on ensuring that portfolio components adhere to established governance processes and policies, promoting accountability, transparency, and alignment with strategic objectives.

Question 82:

In portfolio management, what is the primary objective of a portfolio analysis?

A) To track project schedules

B) To assess individual project performance

C) To evaluate the overall portfolio performance

D) To calculate earned value

Answer: C) To evaluate the overall portfolio performance

Explanation: A portfolio analysis evaluates the overall portfolio performance, considering factors like progress, alignment with objectives, risks, and value generation.

Question 83:

What is the main purpose of conducting a portfolio audit in portfolio management?

A) To track project schedules

B) To assess individual project performance

C) To evaluate the effectiveness of portfolio management practices

D) To calculate earned value

Answer: C) To evaluate the effectiveness of portfolio management practices

Explanation: A portfolio audit assesses the effectiveness of portfolio management practices, processes, and performance, identifying areas for improvement and enhancement.

Question 84:

Which role in portfolio management is responsible for managing and optimizing the utilization of resources across portfolio components?

A) Portfolio manager

B) Governance manager

C) Resource manager

D) Program manager

Answer: C) Resource manager

Explanation: The resource manager is responsible for managing and optimizing the utilization of resources across portfolio components to achieve strategic goals.

Question 85:

In portfolio management, what is the main objective of a portfolio communication plan?

A) To track project schedules

B) To ensure effective communication among stakeholders

C) To allocate project resources

D) To calculate earned value

Answer: B) To ensure effective communication among stakeholders

Explanation: A portfolio communication plan ensures that effective communication takes place among stakeholders, facilitating understanding, alignment, and informed decision-making.

Question 86:

Which type of portfolio management focuses on evaluating the organization's capacity and capability to execute portfolio components successfully?

A) Strategic portfolio management

B) Financial portfolio management

C) Resource portfolio management

D) Value-based portfolio management

Answer: C) Resource portfolio management

Explanation: Resource portfolio management evaluates the organization's capacity and capability to execute portfolio components successfully, ensuring alignment with strategic goals.

Question 87:

What is the primary goal of portfolio value management in portfolio management?

A) To execute project tasks

B) To allocate project resources

C) To calculate earned value

D) To maximize value generation from portfolio components

Answer: D) To maximize value generation from portfolio components

Explanation: Portfolio value management aims to maximize value generation from portfolio components by ensuring alignment with strategic goals and optimizing resource allocation.

Question 88:

In portfolio management, what is the main purpose of a portfolio dashboard?

A) To track project schedules

B) To allocate project resources

C) To visualize the performance and status of portfolio components

D) To calculate earned value

Answer: C) To visualize the performance and status of portfolio components

Explanation: A portfolio dashboard provides a visual representation of the performance and status of portfolio components, enabling stakeholders to make informed decisions and track progress.

Question 89:

Which PfMP domain focuses on defining and implementing the processes for selecting, prioritizing, and authorizing portfolio components?

A) Strategic alignment

B) Governance

C) Portfolio performance

D) Risk management

Answer: A) Strategic alignment

Explanation: The strategic alignment domain focuses on defining and implementing the processes for selecting, prioritizing, and authorizing portfolio components to achieve strategic goals.

Question 90:

What is the main goal of portfolio risk management in portfolio management?

A) To execute project tasks

B) To allocate project resources

C) To track project schedules

D) To identify, assess, and mitigate risks

Answer: D) To identify, assess, and mitigate risks

Explanation: Portfolio risk management involves identifying, assessing, and mitigating risks associated with portfolio components to ensure successful execution and alignment with strategic goals.

Question 91:

Which role in portfolio management is responsible for ensuring that portfolio components adhere to established governance processes and policies?

A) Project manager

B) Portfolio manager

C) Program manager

D) Governance manager

Answer: D) Governance manager

Explanation: The governance manager in portfolio management ensures that portfolio components adhere to established governance processes and policies, promoting accountability and alignment.

Question 92:

What is the main purpose of a portfolio assessment framework in portfolio management?

A) To track project schedules

B) To assess individual project performance

C) To evaluate the overall portfolio performance

D) To allocate project resources

Answer: C) To evaluate the overall portfolio performance

Explanation: A portfolio assessment framework is used to evaluate the overall portfolio performance, considering factors like progress, alignment with objectives, risks, and value generation.

Question 93:

Which PfMP domain focuses on evaluating the financial performance and benefits realization of portfolio components?

A) Strategic alignment

B) Financial management

C) Governance

D) Portfolio performance

Answer: B) Financial management

Explanation: The financial management domain focuses on evaluating the financial performance and benefits realization of portfolio components, ensuring alignment with strategic goals.

Question 94:

In portfolio management, what is the primary objective of a portfolio analysis?

A) To track project schedules

B) To assess individual project performance

C) To evaluate the overall portfolio performance

D) To calculate earned value

Answer: C) To evaluate the overall portfolio performance

Explanation: A portfolio analysis evaluates the overall portfolio performance, including factors such as progress, alignment with objectives, risks, and value generation.

Question 95:

What is the main purpose of conducting a portfolio audit in portfolio management?

A) To track project schedules

B) To assess individual project performance

C) To evaluate the effectiveness of portfolio management practices

D) To calculate earned value

Answer: C) To evaluate the effectiveness of portfolio management practices

Explanation: A portfolio audit assesses the effectiveness of portfolio management practices, processes, and performance, identifying areas for improvement and enhancement.

Question 96:

Which type of portfolio management focuses on evaluating the organization's capacity and capability to execute portfolio components successfully?

A) Strategic portfolio management

B) Financial portfolio management

C) Resource portfolio management

D) Value-based portfolio management

Answer: C) Resource portfolio management

Explanation: Resource portfolio management evaluates the organization's capacity and capability to execute portfolio components successfully, ensuring alignment with strategic goals.

Question 97:

In portfolio management, what is the main objective of a portfolio communication plan?

A) To track project schedules

B) To ensure effective communication among stakeholders

C) To allocate project resources

D) To calculate earned value

Answer: B) To ensure effective communication among stakeholders

Explanation: A portfolio communication plan ensures that effective communication takes place among stakeholders, facilitating understanding, alignment, and informed decision-making.

Question 98:

What is the primary goal of portfolio value management in portfolio management?

A) To execute project tasks

B) To allocate project resources

C) To calculate earned value

D) To maximize value generation from portfolio components

Answer: D) To maximize value generation from portfolio components

Explanation: Portfolio value management aims to maximize value generation from portfolio components by ensuring alignment with strategic goals and optimizing resource allocation.

Question 99:

Which PfMP domain focuses on defining and implementing the processes for selecting, prioritizing, and authorizing portfolio components?

A) Strategic alignment

B) Governance

C) Portfolio performance

D) Risk management

Answer: A) Strategic alignment

Explanation: The strategic alignment domain focuses on defining and implementing the processes for selecting, prioritizing, and authorizing portfolio components to achieve strategic goals.

Question 100:

What is the main goal of portfolio risk management in portfolio management?

A) To execute project tasks

B) To allocate project resources

C) To track project schedules

D) To identify, assess, and mitigate risks

Answer: D) To identify, assess, and mitigate risks

Explanation: Portfolio risk management involves identifying, assessing, and mitigating risks associated with portfolio components to ensure successful execution and alignment with strategic goals.

Question 101:

In portfolio management, what is the primary objective of a portfolio analysis?

A) To track project schedules

B) To assess individual project performance

C) To evaluate the overall portfolio performance

D) To calculate earned value

Answer: C) To evaluate the overall portfolio performance

Explanation: A portfolio analysis evaluates the overall portfolio performance, including factors such as progress, alignment with objectives, risks, and value generation.

Question 102:

What is the main purpose of conducting a portfolio audit in portfolio management?

A) To track project schedules

B) To assess individual project performance

C) To evaluate the effectiveness of portfolio management practices

D) To calculate earned value

Answer: C) To evaluate the effectiveness of portfolio management practices

Explanation: A portfolio audit assesses the effectiveness of portfolio management practices, processes, and performance, identifying areas for improvement and enhancement.

Question 103:

Which type of portfolio management focuses on evaluating the organization's capacity and capability to execute portfolio components successfully?

A) Strategic portfolio management

B) Financial portfolio management

C) Resource portfolio management

D) Value-based portfolio management

Answer: C) Resource portfolio management

Explanation: Resource portfolio management evaluates the organization's capacity and capability to execute portfolio components successfully, ensuring alignment with strategic goals.

Question 104:

In portfolio management, what is the main objective of a portfolio communication plan?

A) To track project schedules

B) To ensure effective communication among stakeholders

C) To allocate project resources

D) To calculate earned value

Answer: B) To ensure effective communication among stakeholders

Explanation: A portfolio communication plan ensures that effective communication takes place among stakeholders, facilitating understanding, alignment, and informed decision-making.

Question 105:

What is the primary goal of portfolio value management in portfolio management?

A) To execute project tasks

B) To allocate project resources

C) To calculate earned value

D) To maximize value generation from portfolio components

Answer: D) To maximize value generation from portfolio components

Explanation: Portfolio value management aims to maximize value generation from portfolio components by ensuring alignment with strategic goals and optimizing resource allocation.

Question 106:

Which PfMP domain focuses on defining and implementing the processes for selecting, prioritizing, and authorizing portfolio components?

A) Strategic alignment

B) Governance

C) Portfolio performance

D) Risk management

Answer: A) Strategic alignment

Explanation: The strategic alignment domain focuses on defining and implementing the processes for selecting, prioritizing, and authorizing portfolio components to achieve strategic goals.

Question 107:

What is the main goal of portfolio risk management in portfolio management?

A) To execute project tasks

B) To allocate project resources

C) To track project schedules

D) To identify, assess, and mitigate risks

Answer: D) To identify, assess, and mitigate risks

Explanation: Portfolio risk management involves identifying, assessing, and mitigating risks associated with portfolio components to ensure successful execution and alignment with strategic goals.

Question 108:

Which role in portfolio management is responsible for ensuring that portfolio components adhere to established governance processes and policies?

A) Project manager

B) Portfolio manager

C) Program manager

D) Governance manager

Answer: D) Governance manager

Explanation: The governance manager in portfolio management ensures that portfolio components adhere to established governance processes and policies, promoting accountability and alignment.

Question 109:

What is the main purpose of a portfolio assessment framework in portfolio management?

A) To track project schedules

B) To assess individual project performance

C) To evaluate the overall portfolio performance

D) To allocate project resources

Answer: C) To evaluate the overall portfolio performance

Explanation: A portfolio assessment framework is used to evaluate the overall portfolio performance, including factors like progress, alignment with objectives, risks, and value generation.

Question 110:

Which PfMP domain focuses on evaluating the financial performance and benefits realization of portfolio components?

A) Strategic alignment

B) Financial management

C) Governance

D) Portfolio performance

Answer: B) Financial management

Explanation: The financial management domain focuses on evaluating the financial performance and benefits realization of portfolio components, ensuring alignment with strategic goals.

Question 111:

What is the main purpose of conducting a portfolio audit in portfolio management?

A) To track project schedules

B) To assess individual project performance

C) To evaluate the effectiveness of portfolio management practices

D) To calculate earned value

Answer: C) To evaluate the effectiveness of portfolio management practices

Explanation: A portfolio audit assesses the effectiveness of portfolio management practices, processes, and performance, identifying areas for improvement and enhancement.

Question 112:

Which type of portfolio management focuses on evaluating the organization's capacity and capability to execute portfolio components successfully?

A) Strategic portfolio management

B) Financial portfolio management

C) Resource portfolio management

D) Value-based portfolio management

Answer: C) Resource portfolio management

Explanation: Resource portfolio management evaluates the organization's capacity and capability to execute portfolio components successfully, ensuring alignment with strategic goals.

Question 113:

In portfolio management, what is the main objective of a portfolio communication plan?

A) To track project schedules

B) To ensure effective communication among stakeholders

C) To allocate project resources

D) To calculate earned value

Answer: B) To ensure effective communication among stakeholders

Explanation: A portfolio communication plan ensures that effective communication takes place among stakeholders, facilitating understanding, alignment, and informed decision-making.

Question 114:

What is the primary goal of portfolio value management in portfolio management?

A) To execute project tasks

B) To allocate project resources

C) To calculate earned value

D) To maximize value generation from portfolio components

Answer: D) To maximize value generation from portfolio components

Explanation: Portfolio value management aims to maximize value generation from portfolio components by ensuring alignment with strategic goals and optimizing resource allocation.

Question 115:

Which PfMP domain focuses on defining and implementing the processes for selecting, prioritizing, and authorizing portfolio components?

A) Strategic alignment

B) Governance

C) Portfolio performance

D) Risk management

Answer: A) Strategic alignment

Explanation: The strategic alignment domain focuses on defining and implementing the processes for selecting, prioritizing, and authorizing portfolio components to achieve strategic goals.

Question 116:

What is the main goal of portfolio risk management in portfolio management?

A) To execute project tasks

B) To allocate project resources

C) To track project schedules

D) To identify, assess, and mitigate risks

Answer: D) To identify, assess, and mitigate risks

Explanation: Portfolio risk management involves identifying, assessing, and mitigating risks associated with portfolio components to ensure successful execution and alignment with strategic goals.

Question 117:

Which role in portfolio management is responsible for ensuring that portfolio components adhere to established governance processes and policies?

A) Project manager

B) Portfolio manager

C) Program manager

D) Governance manager

Answer: D) Governance manager

Explanation: The governance manager in portfolio management ensures that portfolio components adhere to established governance processes and policies, promoting accountability and alignment.

Question 118:

What is the main purpose of a portfolio assessment framework in portfolio management?

A) To track project schedules

B) To assess individual project performance

C) To evaluate the overall portfolio performance

D) To allocate project resources

Answer: C) To evaluate the overall portfolio performance

Explanation: A portfolio assessment framework is used to evaluate the overall portfolio performance, including factors like progress, alignment with objectives, risks, and value generation.

Question 119:

Which PfMP domain focuses on evaluating the financial performance and benefits realization of portfolio components?

A) Strategic alignment

B) Financial management

C) Governance

D) Portfolio performance

Answer: B) Financial management

Explanation: The financial management domain focuses on evaluating the financial performance and benefits realization of portfolio components, ensuring alignment with strategic goals.

Question 120:

What is the main purpose of conducting a portfolio audit in portfolio management?

A) To track project schedules

B) To assess individual project performance

C) To evaluate the effectiveness of portfolio management practices

D) To calculate earned value

Answer: C) To evaluate the effectiveness of portfolio management practices

Explanation: A portfolio audit assesses the effectiveness of portfolio management practices, processes, and performance, identifying areas for improvement and enhancement.

Question 121:

What is the primary purpose of a portfolio roadmap in portfolio management?

A) To allocate project resources

B) To track project schedules

C) To visualize the strategic direction of the portfolio

D) To calculate earned value

Answer: C) To visualize the strategic direction of the portfolio

Explanation: A portfolio roadmap is used to visually depict the strategic direction of the portfolio, helping stakeholders understand the timeline and progression of portfolio components.

Question 122:

Which PfMP domain focuses on establishing and maintaining the portfolio management framework and processes within the organization?

A) Governance

B) Strategic alignment

C) Portfolio performance

D) Risk management

Answer: A) Governance

Explanation: The governance domain focuses on establishing and maintaining the portfolio management framework and processes within the organization to ensure effective portfolio management.

Question 123:

What is the main goal of portfolio resource management in portfolio management?

A) To execute project tasks

B) To allocate project resources

C) To track project schedules

D) To optimize resource allocation for portfolio components

Answer: D) To optimize resource allocation for portfolio components

Explanation: Portfolio resource management aims to optimize resource allocation for portfolio components to ensure successful execution and alignment with strategic goals.

Question 124:

Which role in portfolio management is responsible for monitoring and reporting on the overall performance of the portfolio to key stakeholders?

A) Project manager

B) Portfolio manager

C) Program manager

D) Portfolio analyst

Answer: B) Portfolio manager

Explanation: The portfolio manager is responsible for monitoring and reporting on the overall performance of the portfolio to key stakeholders, ensuring alignment with strategic goals.

Question 125:

What is the primary purpose of a portfolio dashboard in portfolio management?

A) To track project schedules

B) To assess individual project performance

C) To visualize key portfolio performance metrics

D) To allocate project resources

Answer: C) To visualize key portfolio performance metrics

Explanation: A portfolio dashboard is used to visually present key portfolio performance metrics, providing stakeholders with insights into the overall health and progress of the portfolio.

Question 126:

Which PfMP domain focuses on evaluating the benefits realization and value delivery of portfolio components?

A) Strategic alignment

B) Financial management

C) Portfolio performance

D) Governance

Answer: C) Portfolio performance

Explanation: The portfolio performance domain focuses on evaluating the benefits realization and value delivery of portfolio components, ensuring alignment with strategic goals.

Question 127:

What is the main objective of portfolio alignment in portfolio management?

A) To execute project tasks

B) To allocate project resources

C) To track project schedules

D) To ensure that portfolio components align with strategic goals

Answer: D) To ensure that portfolio components align with strategic goals

Explanation: Portfolio alignment involves ensuring that portfolio components align with the organization's strategic goals, maximizing value generation and benefit realization.

Question 128:

Which PfMP domain focuses on identifying, assessing, and managing risks associated with portfolio components?

A) Strategic alignment

B) Risk management

C) Financial management

D) Governance

Answer: B) Risk management

Explanation: The risk management domain focuses on identifying, assessing, and managing risks associated with portfolio components to mitigate potential negative impacts.

Question 129:

What is the primary goal of portfolio governance in portfolio management?

A) To execute project tasks

B) To allocate project resources

C) To track project schedules

D) To ensure effective decision-making and accountability

Answer: D) To ensure effective decision-making and accountability

Explanation: Portfolio governance in portfolio management aims to ensure effective decision-making and accountability across portfolio components, promoting successful execution.

Question 130:

Which role in portfolio management is responsible for establishing the portfolio management framework and defining the processes and standards?

A) Project manager

B) Portfolio manager

C) Program manager

D) Portfolio governance manager

Answer: D) Portfolio governance manager

Explanation: The portfolio governance manager is responsible for establishing the portfolio management framework, defining processes, and setting standards to ensure effective governance.

Question 131:

What is the main purpose of a portfolio benefits register in portfolio management?

A) To track project schedules

B) To assess individual project performance

C) To document the expected benefits and outcomes of portfolio components

D) To allocate project resources

Answer: C) To document the expected benefits and outcomes of portfolio components

Explanation: A portfolio benefits register documents the expected benefits and outcomes of portfolio components, facilitating benefits realization tracking and alignment with strategic goals.

Question 132:

Which PfMP domain focuses on evaluating the alignment of portfolio components with the organization's strategic objectives and priorities?

A) Portfolio performance

B) Strategic alignment

C) Financial management

D) Governance

Answer: B) Strategic alignment

Explanation: The strategic alignment domain focuses on evaluating the alignment of portfolio components with the organization's strategic objectives and priorities.

Question 133:

What is the primary goal of portfolio financial management in portfolio management?

A) To execute project tasks

B) To allocate project resources

C) To calculate earned value

D) To optimize financial investment in portfolio components

Answer: D) To optimize financial investment in portfolio components

Explanation: Portfolio financial management aims to optimize financial investment in portfolio components to ensure alignment with strategic goals and value generation.

Question 134:

Which role in portfolio management is responsible for ensuring that portfolio components are executed according to established processes and standards?

A) Project manager

B) Portfolio manager

C) Program manager

D) Portfolio governance manager

Answer: A) Project manager

Explanation: The project manager is responsible for ensuring that portfolio components are executed according to established processes and standards, contributing to successful delivery.

Question 135:

What is the main purpose of portfolio component evaluation in portfolio management?

A) To track project schedules

B) To assess individual project performance

C) To evaluate the alignment of portfolio components with strategic goals

D) To allocate project resources

Answer: B) To assess individual project performance

Explanation: Portfolio component evaluation involves assessing the individual performance of portfolio components to ensure alignment with strategic goals and identify areas for improvement.

Question 136:

Which PfMP domain focuses on defining and implementing the processes for selecting and authorizing portfolio components?

A) Financial management

B) Governance

C) Strategic alignment

D) Portfolio performance

Answer: C) Strategic alignment

Explanation: The strategic alignment domain focuses on defining and implementing the processes for selecting and authorizing portfolio components to achieve strategic goals.

Question 137:

What is the main objective of portfolio risk management in portfolio management?

A) To execute project tasks

B) To allocate project resources

C) To track project schedules

D) To identify, assess, and mitigate risks

Answer: D) To identify, assess, and mitigate risks

Explanation: Portfolio risk management involves identifying, assessing, and mitigating risks associated with portfolio components to ensure successful execution and alignment with strategic goals.

Question 138:

Which role in portfolio management is responsible for defining the strategic goals and objectives of the portfolio?

A) Project manager

B) Portfolio manager

C) Program manager

D) Chief Executive Officer (CEO)

Answer: D) Chief Executive Officer (CEO)

Explanation: The Chief Executive Officer (CEO) or an executive role is responsible for defining the strategic goals and objectives of the portfolio, ensuring alignment with the organization's vision.

Question 139:

What is the primary purpose of a portfolio steering committee in portfolio management?

A) To track project schedules

B) To assess individual project performance

C) To provide oversight and direction for the portfolio

D) To allocate project resources

Answer: C) To provide oversight and direction for the portfolio

Explanation: A portfolio steering committee provides oversight and direction for the portfolio, ensuring alignment with strategic goals and informed decision-making.

Question 140:

Which PfMP domain focuses on evaluating the overall financial health of portfolio components and ensuring financial alignment with strategic goals?

A) Financial management

B) Strategic alignment

C) Governance

D) Portfolio performance

Answer: A) Financial management

Explanation: The financial management domain focuses on evaluating the overall financial health of portfolio components and ensuring financial alignment with strategic goals.

Question 141:

In portfolio management, what is the primary objective of risk response planning for portfolio components?

A) To avoid all risks

B) To accept all risks

C) To identify all risks

D) To develop strategies for addressing identified risks

Answer: D) To develop strategies for addressing identified risks

Explanation: Risk response planning in portfolio management involves developing strategies to address identified risks, ensuring effective risk mitigation and alignment with strategic objectives.

Question 142:

Which PfMP domain focuses on evaluating the performance and effectiveness of the portfolio management processes and practices?

A) Portfolio performance

B) Governance

C) Financial management

D) Strategic alignment

Answer: A) Portfolio performance

Explanation: The portfolio performance domain focuses on evaluating the performance and effectiveness of the portfolio management processes and practices to ensure continuous improvement.

Question 143:

What is the main purpose of portfolio component selection in portfolio management?

A) To execute project tasks

B) To allocate project resources

C) To identify potential portfolio components

D) To choose the most valuable and strategic portfolio components

Answer: D) To choose the most valuable and strategic portfolio components

Explanation: Portfolio component selection involves choosing the most valuable and strategic portfolio components that align with the organization's goals and priorities.

Question 144:

Which role in portfolio management is responsible for ensuring that portfolio components are executed according to the organization's standards and policies?

A) Project manager

B) Portfolio manager

C) Program manager

D) Compliance officer

Answer: B) Portfolio manager

Explanation: The portfolio manager is responsible for ensuring that portfolio components are executed according to the organization's standards and policies, ensuring consistency and compliance.

Question 145:

What is the primary objective of portfolio change management in portfolio management?

A) To execute project tasks

B) To allocate project resources

C) To track project schedules

D) To manage changes to portfolio components and their impacts

Answer: D) To manage changes to portfolio components and their impacts

Explanation: Portfolio change management involves managing changes to portfolio components and their impacts to ensure that changes are effectively implemented and aligned with strategic goals.

Question 146:

Which PfMP domain focuses on assessing the financial feasibility and return on investment of portfolio components?

A) Financial management

B) Governance

C) Portfolio performance

D) Strategic alignment

Answer: A) Financial management

Explanation: The financial management domain focuses on assessing the financial feasibility and return on investment of portfolio components to ensure alignment with strategic objectives.

Question 147:

What is the primary goal of portfolio component prioritization in portfolio management?

A) To execute project tasks

B) To allocate project resources

C) To identify potential portfolio components

D) To determine the order of execution for portfolio components

Answer: D) To determine the order of execution for portfolio components

Explanation: Portfolio component prioritization involves determining the order of execution for portfolio components based on their strategic importance and value.

Question 148:

Which role in portfolio management is responsible for evaluating the overall alignment of portfolio components with the organization's strategic goals?

A) Project manager

B) Portfolio manager

C) Program manager

D) Chief Financial Officer (CFO)

Answer: B) Portfolio manager

Explanation: The portfolio manager is responsible for evaluating the overall alignment of portfolio components with the organization's strategic goals, ensuring value generation.

Question 149:

What is the main purpose of portfolio investment management in portfolio management?

A) To execute project tasks

B) To allocate project resources

C) To track project schedules

D) To optimize the allocation of resources and investments for portfolio components

Answer: D) To optimize the allocation of resources and investments for portfolio components

Explanation: Portfolio investment management aims to optimize the allocation of resources and investments for portfolio components to achieve strategic goals and maximize value.

Question 150:

Which PfMP domain focuses on defining and implementing processes to ensure that portfolio components are aligned with the organization's strategy and goals?

A) Governance

B) Financial management

C) Strategic alignment

D) Portfolio performance

Answer: C) Strategic alignment

Explanation: The strategic alignment domain focuses on defining and implementing processes to ensure that portfolio components are aligned with the organization's strategy and goals.

Question 151:

What is the primary objective of portfolio component assessment in portfolio management?

A) To track project schedules

B) To assess individual project performance

C) To evaluate the alignment of portfolio components with strategic goals

D) To allocate project resources

Answer: B) To assess individual project performance

Explanation: Portfolio component assessment involves assessing the individual performance of portfolio components to ensure alignment with strategic goals and identify areas for improvement.

Question 152:

Which role in portfolio management is responsible for making key decisions regarding the overall composition of the portfolio?

A) Project manager

B) Portfolio manager

C) Program manager

D) Chief Executive Officer (CEO)

Answer: B) Portfolio manager

Explanation: The portfolio manager is responsible for making key decisions regarding the overall composition of the portfolio, ensuring alignment with strategic objectives.

Question 153:

What is the main purpose of portfolio benefits management in portfolio management?

A) To execute project tasks

B) To allocate project resources

C) To track project schedules

D) To ensure that portfolio components deliver expected benefits and value

Answer: D) To ensure that portfolio components deliver expected benefits and value

Explanation: Portfolio benefits management focuses on ensuring that portfolio components deliver expected benefits and value to the organization, contributing to strategic objectives.

Question 154:

Which PfMP domain focuses on establishing processes to monitor and report the performance and progress of portfolio components?

A) Portfolio performance

B) Governance

C) Financial management

D) Strategic alignment

Answer: A) Portfolio performance

Explanation: The portfolio performance domain focuses on establishing processes to monitor and report the performance and progress of portfolio components, enabling informed decision-making.

Question 155:

What is the primary goal of portfolio risk management in portfolio management?

A) To execute project tasks

B) To allocate project resources

C) To track project schedules

D) To identify, assess, and mitigate risks

Answer: D) To identify, assess, and mitigate risks

Explanation: Portfolio risk management involves identifying, assessing, and mitigating risks associated with portfolio components to ensure successful execution and alignment with strategic goals.

Question 156:

Which role in portfolio management is responsible for ensuring that portfolio components are executed according to established processes and standards?

A) Project manager

B) Portfolio manager

C) Program manager

D) Portfolio governance manager

Answer: A) Project manager

Explanation: The project manager is responsible for ensuring that portfolio components are executed according to established processes and standards, contributing to successful delivery.

Question 157:

What is the primary purpose of portfolio component evaluation in portfolio management?

A) To track project schedules

B) To assess individual project performance

C) To evaluate the alignment of portfolio components with strategic goals

D) To allocate project resources

Answer: B) To assess individual project performance

Explanation: Portfolio component evaluation involves assessing the individual performance of portfolio components to ensure alignment with strategic goals and identify areas for improvement.

Question 158:

Which PfMP domain focuses on evaluating the overall financial health of portfolio components and ensuring financial alignment with strategic goals?

A) Financial management

B) Strategic alignment

C) Governance

D) Portfolio performance

Answer: A) Financial management

Explanation: The financial management domain focuses on evaluating the overall financial health of portfolio components and ensuring financial alignment with strategic goals.

Question 159:

What is the main objective of portfolio component selection in portfolio management?

A) To execute project tasks

B) To allocate project resources

C) To identify potential portfolio components

D) To choose the most valuable and strategic portfolio components

Answer: D) To choose the most valuable and strategic portfolio components

Explanation: Portfolio component selection involves choosing the most valuable and strategic portfolio components that align with the organization's goals and priorities.

Question 160:

Which role in portfolio management is responsible for evaluating the overall alignment of portfolio components with the organization's strategic goals?

A) Project manager

B) Portfolio manager

C) Program manager

D) Chief Financial Officer (CFO)

Answer: B) Portfolio manager

Explanation: The portfolio manager is responsible for evaluating the overall alignment of portfolio components with the organization's strategic goals, ensuring value generation.

Question 161:

What is the main focus of portfolio component governance in portfolio management?

A) Financial management

B) Risk management

C) Oversight and decision-making for portfolio components

D) Allocation of project resources

Answer: C) Oversight and decision-making for portfolio components

Explanation: Portfolio component governance involves providing oversight and making decisions related to the execution of portfolio components to ensure alignment with strategic goals.

Question 162:

Which PfMP domain focuses on defining and implementing processes to monitor and control changes to portfolio components?

A) Portfolio performance

B) Governance

C) Financial management

D) Strategic alignment

Answer: B) Governance

Explanation: The governance domain focuses on defining and implementing processes to monitor and control changes to portfolio components, ensuring alignment with organizational policies and objectives.

Question 163:

What is the primary goal of portfolio communication management in portfolio management?

A) To execute project tasks

B) To allocate project resources

C) To communicate project schedules

D) To ensure effective communication among stakeholders for portfolio components

Answer: D) To ensure effective communication among stakeholders for portfolio components

Explanation: Portfolio communication management aims to ensure effective communication among stakeholders for portfolio components, facilitating informed decision-making and collaboration.

Question 164:

Which role in portfolio management is responsible for establishing the overall governance framework for portfolio components?

A) Project manager

B) Portfolio manager

C) Program manager

D) Chief Governance Officer

Answer: B) Portfolio manager

Explanation: The portfolio manager is responsible for establishing the overall governance framework for portfolio components, ensuring adherence to organizational policies and standards.

Question 165:

What is the main purpose of portfolio performance measurement in portfolio management?

A) To execute project tasks

B) To allocate project resources

C) To track project schedules

D) To assess the performance and progress of portfolio components

Answer: D) To assess the performance and progress of portfolio components

Explanation: Portfolio performance measurement involves assessing the performance and progress of portfolio components to ensure alignment with strategic goals and identify areas for improvement.

Question 166:

Which PfMP domain focuses on defining and implementing processes to ensure that portfolio components deliver expected benefits and value?

A) Financial management

B) Portfolio performance

C) Governance

D) Benefits realization management

Answer: D) Benefits realization management

Explanation: The benefits realization management domain focuses on defining and implementing processes to ensure that portfolio components deliver expected benefits and value to the organization.

Question 167:

What is the primary objective of portfolio investment prioritization in portfolio management?

A) To execute project tasks

B) To allocate project resources

C) To track project schedules

D) To determine the order of investment for portfolio components

Answer: D) To determine the order of investment for portfolio components

Explanation: Portfolio investment prioritization involves determining the order of investment for portfolio components based on their strategic value and potential benefits.

Question 168:

Which role in portfolio management is responsible for ensuring that portfolio components are aligned with the organization's strategic goals and objectives?

A) Project manager

B) Portfolio manager

C) Program manager

D) Chief Strategy Officer

Answer: B) Portfolio manager

Explanation: The portfolio manager is responsible for ensuring that portfolio components are aligned with the organization's strategic goals and objectives, driving value realization.

Question 169:

What is the main focus of portfolio component dependency management in portfolio management?

A) Financial management

B) Resource allocation

C) Identifying project risks

D) Managing relationships and interactions among portfolio components

Answer: D) Managing relationships and interactions among portfolio components

Explanation: Portfolio component dependency management involves managing relationships and interactions among portfolio components to ensure successful execution and alignment with strategic goals.

Question 170:

Which PfMP domain focuses on evaluating the overall alignment of portfolio components with the organization's strategic goals and objectives?

A) Governance

B) Financial management

C) Strategic alignment

D) Portfolio performance

Answer: C) Strategic alignment

Explanation: The strategic alignment domain focuses on evaluating the overall alignment of portfolio components with the organization's strategic goals and objectives.

PRACTICE TEST - 2

Question 171:

What is the primary objective of portfolio change control in portfolio management?

A) To execute project tasks

B) To allocate project resources

C) To manage changes to portfolio components and their impacts

D) To identify potential portfolio components

Answer: C) To manage changes to portfolio components and their impacts

Explanation: Portfolio change control involves managing changes to portfolio components and their impacts to ensure that changes are effectively implemented and aligned with strategic goals.

Question 172:

Which role in portfolio management is responsible for defining and implementing portfolio governance processes and structures?

A) Project manager

B) Portfolio manager

C) Program manager

D) Chief Governance Officer

Answer: D) Chief Governance Officer

Explanation: The Chief Governance Officer is responsible for defining and implementing portfolio governance processes and structures to ensure effective decision-making and alignment with organizational objectives.

Question 173:

What is the main goal of portfolio component integration in portfolio management?

A) To execute project tasks

B) To allocate project resources

C) To manage project schedules

D) To ensure that portfolio components work together cohesively

Answer: D) To ensure that portfolio components work together cohesively

Explanation: Portfolio component integration aims to ensure that portfolio components work together cohesively, enabling the organization to achieve its strategic objectives.

Question 174:

Which PfMP domain focuses on evaluating the financial performance of portfolio components and their contribution to strategic goals?

A) Portfolio performance

B) Financial management

C) Governance

D) Strategic alignment

Answer: B) Financial management

Explanation: The financial management domain focuses on evaluating the financial performance of portfolio components and their contribution to strategic goals.

Question 175:

What is the primary purpose of portfolio component closure in portfolio management?

A) To execute project tasks

B) To allocate project resources

C) To track project schedules

D) To formally close portfolio components and assess their outcomes

Answer: D) To formally close portfolio components and assess their outcomes

Explanation: Portfolio component closure involves formally closing portfolio components and assessing their outcomes to determine whether strategic goals were achieved and lessons learned.

Question 176:

Which role in portfolio management is responsible for defining and implementing processes to manage the overall risk exposure of the portfolio?

A) Project manager

B) Portfolio manager

C) Program manager

D) Chief Risk Officer

Answer: D) Chief Risk Officer

Explanation: The Chief Risk Officer is responsible for defining and implementing processes to manage the overall risk exposure of the portfolio, ensuring risk mitigation and alignment with organizational risk appetite.

Question 177:

What is the primary objective of portfolio performance evaluation in portfolio management?

A) To execute project tasks

B) To allocate project resources

C) To track project schedules

D) To assess the overall performance and progress of the portfolio

Answer: D) To assess the overall performance and progress of the portfolio

Explanation: Portfolio performance evaluation involves assessing the overall performance and progress of the portfolio to ensure alignment with strategic goals and identify areas for improvement.

Question 178:

Which PfMP domain focuses on establishing processes to ensure that portfolio components are executed according to established guidelines?

A) Financial management

B) Portfolio performance

C) Governance

D) Benefits realization management

Answer: C) Governance

Explanation: The governance domain focuses on establishing processes to ensure that portfolio components are executed according to established guidelines, policies, and standards.

Question 179:

What is the main purpose of portfolio component coordination in portfolio management?

A) To execute project tasks

B) To allocate project resources

C) To manage project schedules

D) To ensure that portfolio components are aligned and integrated

Answer: D) To ensure that portfolio components are aligned and integrated

Explanation: Portfolio component coordination involves ensuring that portfolio components are aligned and integrated to achieve overall strategic objectives cohesively.

Question 180:

Which role in portfolio management is responsible for identifying potential portfolio components that align with the organization's strategic goals?

A) Project manager

B) Portfolio manager

C) Program manager

D) Chief Strategy Officer

Answer: D) Chief Strategy Officer

Explanation: The Chief Strategy Officer is responsible for identifying potential portfolio components that align with the organization's strategic goals, driving the organization's direction.

Question 181:

In portfolio management, what is the primary goal of risk management for portfolio components?

A) To allocate project resources effectively

B) To track project schedules accurately

C) To identify and mitigate potential risks to portfolio components

D) To ensure that portfolio components are executed on time

Answer: C) To identify and mitigate potential risks to portfolio components

Explanation: The primary goal of risk management for portfolio components is to identify and mitigate potential risks that could impact the successful execution of the portfolio components and the achievement of strategic objectives.

Question 182:

Which PfMP domain focuses on establishing processes for evaluating the overall performance and benefits realization of portfolio components?

A) Financial management

B) Portfolio performance

C) Governance

D) Benefits realization management

Answer: D) Benefits realization management

Explanation: The benefits realization management domain focuses on establishing processes for evaluating the overall performance and benefits realization of portfolio components, ensuring alignment with strategic goals.

Question 183:

What is the main purpose of portfolio component resource optimization in portfolio management?

A) To execute project tasks efficiently

B) To track project schedules accurately

C) To ensure that the right resources are allocated to portfolio components

D) To communicate project progress to stakeholders

Answer: C) To ensure that the right resources are allocated to portfolio components

Explanation: Portfolio component resource optimization aims to ensure that the right resources, including people, budget, and materials, are allocated to portfolio components to achieve strategic objectives efficiently.

Question 184:

Which role in portfolio management is responsible for overseeing the performance and alignment of individual projects and programs within the portfolio?

A) Project manager

B) Portfolio manager

C) Program manager

D) Chief Operations Officer

Answer: C) Program manager

Explanation: The program manager is responsible for overseeing the performance and alignment of individual projects and programs within the portfolio, ensuring they contribute to the overall strategic goals.

Question 185:

What is the primary focus of portfolio component benefits realization in portfolio management?

A) Allocating project resources

B) Tracking project schedules

C) Achieving the expected benefits and value from portfolio components

D) Monitoring portfolio performance

Answer: C) Achieving the expected benefits and value from portfolio components

Explanation: Portfolio component benefits realization focuses on achieving the expected benefits and value from portfolio components, ensuring alignment with strategic goals and organizational objectives.

Question 186:

Which PfMP domain focuses on ensuring that portfolio components are executed within defined constraints and guidelines?

A) Financial management

B) Portfolio performance

C) Governance

D) Resource management

Answer: C) Governance

Explanation: The governance domain focuses on ensuring that portfolio components are executed within defined constraints and guidelines, facilitating effective decision-making and alignment with organizational objectives.

Question 187:

What is the main objective of portfolio component selection in portfolio management?

A) To allocate project resources

B) To track project schedules

C) To identify potential portfolio components

D) To choose the most valuable portfolio components that align with strategic goals

Answer: D) To choose the most valuable portfolio components that align with strategic goals

Explanation: The main objective of portfolio component selection is to choose the most valuable portfolio components that align with strategic goals and provide the greatest potential benefits to the organization.

Question 188:

Which role in portfolio management is responsible for ensuring that portfolio components are executed according to established guidelines and processes?

A) Project manager

B) Portfolio manager

C) Program manager

D) Chief Compliance Officer

Answer: D) Chief Compliance Officer

Explanation: The Chief Compliance Officer is responsible for ensuring that portfolio components are executed according to established guidelines and processes, ensuring compliance with relevant regulations and standards.

Question 189:

What is the primary goal of portfolio component performance measurement in portfolio management?

A) Allocating project resources effectively

B) Tracking project schedules accurately

C) Assessing the performance and progress of portfolio components

D) Identifying potential risks to portfolio components

Answer: C) Assessing the performance and progress of portfolio components

Explanation: The primary goal of portfolio component performance measurement is to assess the performance and progress of portfolio components to ensure alignment with strategic goals and identify areas for improvement.

Question 190:

Which PfMP domain focuses on defining and implementing processes for effectively allocating and managing the resources of portfolio components?

A) Financial management

B) Resource management

C) Governance

D) Portfolio performance

Answer: B) Resource management

Explanation: The resource management domain focuses on defining and implementing processes for effectively allocating and managing the resources of portfolio components to ensure successful execution.

Question 191:

What is the main focus of portfolio component prioritization in portfolio management?

A) Allocating project resources efficiently

B) Tracking project schedules accurately

C) Determining the order of investment for portfolio components

D) Identifying potential risks to portfolio components

Answer: C) Determining the order of investment for portfolio components

Explanation: Portfolio component prioritization focuses on determining the order of investment for portfolio components based on their strategic value and potential benefits to the organization.

Question 192:

Which role in portfolio management is responsible for ensuring that portfolio components contribute to the overall strategic goals of the organization?

A) Project manager

B) Portfolio manager

C) Program manager

D) Chief Strategy Officer

Answer: B) Portfolio manager

Explanation: The portfolio manager is responsible for ensuring that portfolio components contribute to the overall strategic goals of the organization and are aligned with its strategic direction.

Question 193:

What is the primary purpose of portfolio component alignment in portfolio management?

A) To execute project tasks efficiently

B) To allocate project resources effectively

C) To ensure that portfolio components are aligned with strategic goals

D) To monitor project progress and performance

Answer: C) To ensure that portfolio components are aligned with strategic goals

Explanation: Portfolio component alignment involves ensuring that portfolio components are aligned with the organization's strategic goals and direction to maximize their value and contribution.

Question 194:

Which PfMP domain focuses on establishing processes for effective communication and reporting within the portfolio management framework?

A) Financial management

B) Governance

C) Portfolio performance

D) Communication management

Answer: D) Communication management

Explanation: The communication management domain focuses on establishing processes for effective communication and reporting within the portfolio management framework, ensuring stakeholders are informed and engaged.

Question 195:

What is the main objective of portfolio component evaluation in portfolio management?

A) Allocating project resources

B) Tracking project schedules

C) Assessing the value and benefits of portfolio components

D) Identifying potential risks to portfolio components

Answer: C) Assessing the value and benefits of portfolio components

Explanation: The main objective of portfolio component evaluation is to assess the value and benefits of portfolio components to determine their alignment with strategic goals and their potential contribution.

Question 196:

In portfolio management, what is the purpose of portfolio component integration?

A) To execute project tasks

B) To allocate project resources

C) To manage project schedules

D) To ensure that portfolio components work together cohesively

Answer: D) To ensure that portfolio components work together cohesively

Explanation: Portfolio component integration aims to ensure that portfolio components work together cohesively, enabling the organization to achieve its strategic objectives.

Question 197:

Which PfMP domain focuses on evaluating the financial performance of portfolio components and their contribution to strategic goals?

A) Portfolio performance

B) Financial management

C) Governance

D) Strategic alignment

Answer: B) Financial management

Explanation: The financial management domain focuses on evaluating the financial performance of portfolio components and their contribution to strategic goals.

Question 198:

What is the primary purpose of portfolio component closure in portfolio management?

A) To execute project tasks

B) To allocate project resources

C) To track project schedules

D) To formally close portfolio components and assess their outcomes

Answer: D) To formally close portfolio components and assess their outcomes

Explanation: Portfolio component closure involves formally closing portfolio components and assessing their outcomes to determine whether strategic goals were achieved and lessons learned.

Question 199:

Which role in portfolio management is responsible for defining and implementing processes to manage the overall risk exposure of the portfolio?

A) Project manager

B) Portfolio manager

C) Program manager

D) Chief Risk Officer

Answer: D) Chief Risk Officer

Explanation: The Chief Risk Officer is responsible for defining and implementing processes to manage the overall risk exposure of the portfolio, ensuring risk mitigation and alignment with organizational risk appetite.

Question 200:

What is the primary objective of portfolio performance evaluation in portfolio management?

A) To execute project tasks

B) To allocate project resources

C) To track project schedules

D) To assess the overall performance and progress of the portfolio

Answer: D) To assess the overall performance and progress of the portfolio

Explanation: Portfolio performance evaluation involves assessing the overall performance and progress of the portfolio to ensure alignment with strategic goals and identify areas for improvement.

Question 201:

What is the primary purpose of portfolio component governance in portfolio management?

A) To execute project tasks efficiently

B) To allocate project resources effectively

C) To ensure that portfolio components are aligned with strategic goals

D) To establish processes for effective decision-making and oversight

Answer: D) To establish processes for effective decision-making and oversight

Explanation: Portfolio component governance focuses on establishing processes for effective decision-making and oversight to ensure that portfolio components align with strategic goals and are executed successfully.

Question 202:

Which PfMP domain focuses on defining and implementing processes to ensure that portfolio components are executed efficiently and effectively?

A) Financial management

B) Portfolio performance

C) Resource management

D) Governance

Answer: B) Portfolio performance

Explanation: The portfolio performance domain focuses on defining and implementing processes to ensure that portfolio components are executed efficiently and effectively to achieve strategic objectives.

Question 203:

What is the main objective of portfolio component execution in portfolio management?

A) To allocate project resources

B) To track project schedules

C) To ensure that portfolio components are executed according to established guidelines

D) To identify potential risks to portfolio components

Answer: C) To ensure that portfolio components are executed according to established guidelines

Explanation: The main objective of portfolio component execution is to ensure that portfolio components are executed according to established guidelines and processes, aligning with strategic goals.

Question 204:

Which role in portfolio management is responsible for evaluating the alignment of portfolio components with the organization's strategic goals?

A) Project manager

B) Portfolio manager

C) Program manager

D) Chief Strategy Officer

Answer: D) Chief Strategy Officer

Explanation: The Chief Strategy Officer is responsible for evaluating the alignment of portfolio components with the organization's strategic goals and making strategic decisions.

Question 205:

What is the primary focus of portfolio component closure in portfolio management?

A) Allocating project resources

B) Tracking project schedules

C) Assessing the outcomes and value delivered by portfolio components

D) Identifying potential risks to portfolio components

Answer: C) Assessing the outcomes and value delivered by portfolio components

Explanation: The primary focus of portfolio component closure is to assess the outcomes and value delivered by portfolio components, determining their contribution to strategic goals and lessons learned.

Question 206:

Which PfMP domain focuses on establishing processes for effectively managing the financial resources of portfolio components?

A) Financial management

B) Resource management

C) Governance

D) Portfolio performance

Answer: A) Financial management

Explanation: The financial management domain focuses on establishing processes for effectively managing the financial resources of portfolio components, ensuring alignment with strategic goals.

Question 207:

In portfolio management, what is the purpose of portfolio component integration management?

A) To execute project tasks

B) To allocate project resources

C) To manage project schedules

D) To ensure that portfolio components work together cohesively

Answer: D) To ensure that portfolio components work together cohesively

Explanation: Portfolio component integration management aims to ensure that portfolio components work together cohesively to achieve the organization's strategic goals.

Question 208:

What is the main purpose of portfolio component selection in portfolio management?

A) To allocate project resources

B) To track project schedules

C) To identify potential portfolio components

D) To choose the most valuable portfolio components that align with strategic goals

Answer: D) To choose the most valuable portfolio components that align with strategic goals

Explanation: The main purpose of portfolio component selection is to choose the most valuable portfolio components that align with strategic goals and provide the highest potential benefits to the organization.

Question 209:

Which role in portfolio management is responsible for ensuring that portfolio components are executed according to established guidelines and processes?

A) Project manager

B) Portfolio manager

C) Program manager

D) Chief Compliance Officer

Answer: D) Chief Compliance Officer

Explanation: The Chief Compliance Officer is responsible for ensuring that portfolio components are executed according to established guidelines and processes, ensuring compliance with relevant regulations and standards.

Question 210:

What is the primary goal of portfolio component resource optimization in portfolio management?

A) To execute project tasks efficiently

B) To track project schedules accurately

C) To ensure that the right resources are allocated to portfolio components

D) To communicate project progress to stakeholders

Answer: C) To ensure that the right resources are allocated to portfolio components

Explanation: The primary goal of portfolio component resource optimization is to ensure that the right resources, including people, budget, and materials, are allocated to portfolio components to achieve strategic objectives efficiently.

Question 211:

Which PfMP domain focuses on defining and implementing processes for effectively allocating and managing the resources of portfolio components?

A) Financial management

B) Resource management

C) Governance

D) Portfolio performance

Answer: B) Resource management

Explanation: The resource management domain focuses on defining and implementing processes for effectively allocating and managing the resources of portfolio components to ensure successful execution.

Question 212:

What is the primary objective of portfolio component prioritization in portfolio management?

A) To execute project tasks

B) To allocate project resources

C) To identify potential portfolio components

D) To choose the most valuable portfolio components based on strategic alignment

Answer: D) To choose the most valuable portfolio components based on strategic alignment

Explanation: The primary objective of portfolio component prioritization is to choose the most valuable portfolio components based on their strategic alignment and potential contribution to the organization's goals.

Question 213:

In portfolio management, what is the purpose of portfolio component monitoring and control?

A) To execute project tasks

B) To allocate project resources

C) To track project schedules

D) To ensure that portfolio components are on track and aligned with strategic goals

Answer: D) To ensure that portfolio components are on track and aligned with strategic goals

Explanation: Portfolio component monitoring and control aims to ensure that portfolio components are on track, performing according to plan, and aligned with strategic goals.

Question 214:

What is the primary focus of portfolio component evaluation in portfolio management?

A) Allocating project resources

B) Tracking project schedules

C) Assessing the outcomes and value delivered by portfolio components

D) Identifying potential risks to portfolio components

Answer: C) Assessing the outcomes and value delivered by portfolio components

Explanation: The primary focus of portfolio component evaluation is to assess the outcomes and value delivered by portfolio components, determining their contribution to strategic goals and lessons learned.

Question 215:

Which PfMP domain focuses on defining and implementing processes for effective risk management within the portfolio?

A) Financial management

B) Resource management

C) Governance

D) Risk management

Answer: D) Risk management

Explanation: The risk management domain focuses on defining and implementing processes for effective risk management within the portfolio, identifying and mitigating risks that may impact strategic goals.

Question 216:

What is the primary purpose of portfolio component execution management in portfolio management?

A) To allocate project resources

B) To track project schedules

C) To ensure that portfolio components are executed according to established guidelines

D) To identify potential risks to portfolio components

Answer: C) To ensure that portfolio components are executed according to established guidelines

Explanation: Portfolio component execution management focuses on ensuring that portfolio components are executed according to established guidelines and processes, aligning with strategic goals.

Question 217:

Which role in portfolio management is responsible for evaluating the financial feasibility and viability of portfolio components?

A) Project manager

B) Portfolio manager

C) Program manager

D) Chief Financial Officer

Answer: D) Chief Financial Officer

Explanation: The Chief Financial Officer is responsible for evaluating the financial feasibility and viability of portfolio components, ensuring alignment with the organization's financial goals.

Question 218:

What is the main objective of portfolio component integration management in portfolio management?

A) To execute project tasks

B) To allocate project resources

C) To manage project schedules

D) To ensure that portfolio components work together cohesively

Answer: D) To ensure that portfolio components work together cohesively

Explanation: The main objective of portfolio component integration management is to ensure that portfolio components work together cohesively to achieve the organization's strategic goals.

Question 219:

In portfolio management, what is the purpose of portfolio component selection management?

A) To execute project tasks

B) To allocate project resources

C) To manage project schedules

D) To choose the most valuable portfolio components that align with strategic goals

Answer: D) To choose the most valuable portfolio components that align with strategic goals

Explanation: Portfolio component selection management focuses on choosing the most valuable portfolio components that align with strategic goals and provide the highest potential benefits to the organization.

Question 220:

What is the primary focus of portfolio component governance in portfolio management?

A) To execute project tasks

B) To allocate project resources

C) To ensure that portfolio components are aligned with strategic goals

D) To establish processes for effective decision-making and oversight

Answer: D) To establish processes for effective decision-making and oversight

Explanation: Portfolio component governance focuses on establishing processes for effective decision-making and oversight to ensure that portfolio components align with strategic goals and are executed successfully.

Question 221:

What is the primary objective of portfolio component closure management in portfolio management?

A) To execute project tasks

B) To allocate project resources

C) To assess the outcomes and value delivered by portfolio components

D) To identify potential risks to portfolio components

Answer: C) To assess the outcomes and value delivered by portfolio components

Explanation: The primary objective of portfolio component closure management is to assess the outcomes and value delivered by portfolio components, determining their contribution to strategic goals and lessons learned.

Question 222:

Which PfMP domain focuses on defining and implementing processes for effective communication with stakeholders of portfolio components?

A) Stakeholder engagement

B) Governance

C) Portfolio performance

D) Resource management

Answer: A) Stakeholder engagement

Explanation: The stakeholder engagement domain focuses on defining and implementing processes for effective communication with stakeholders of portfolio components to ensure their involvement and support.

Question 223:

What is the main purpose of portfolio component resource management in portfolio management?

A) To execute project tasks

B) To track project schedules

C) To ensure that the right resources are allocated to portfolio components

D) To communicate project progress to stakeholders

Answer: C) To ensure that the right resources are allocated to portfolio components

Explanation: The main purpose of portfolio component resource management is to ensure that the right resources, including people, budget, and materials, are allocated to portfolio components to achieve strategic objectives efficiently.

Question 224:

Which role in portfolio management is responsible for defining and implementing processes to manage the risks associated with portfolio components?

A) Project manager

B) Portfolio manager

C) Risk manager

D) Chief Risk Officer

Answer: D) Chief Risk Officer

Explanation: The Chief Risk Officer is responsible for defining and implementing processes to manage the risks associated with portfolio components, ensuring risk mitigation and compliance.

Question 225:

What is the primary focus of portfolio component evaluation management in portfolio management?

A) Allocating project resources

B) Tracking project schedules

C) Assessing the outcomes and value delivered by portfolio components

D) Identifying potential risks to portfolio components

Answer: C) Assessing the outcomes and value delivered by portfolio components

Explanation: The primary focus of portfolio component evaluation management is to assess the outcomes and value delivered by portfolio components, determining their contribution to strategic goals and lessons learned.

Question 226:

Which PfMP domain focuses on defining and implementing processes for effective change management within the portfolio?

A) Financial management

B) Resource management

C) Governance

D) Change management

Answer: D) Change management

Explanation: The change management domain focuses on defining and implementing processes for effective change management within the portfolio, ensuring successful adoption of changes.

Question 227:

In portfolio management, what is the purpose of portfolio component integration management?

A) To execute project tasks

B) To allocate project resources

C) To manage project schedules

D) To ensure that portfolio components work together cohesively

Answer: D) To ensure that portfolio components work together cohesively

Explanation: Portfolio component integration management aims to ensure that portfolio components work together cohesively to achieve the organization's strategic goals.

Question 228:

What is the main purpose of portfolio component selection evaluation in portfolio management?

A) To allocate project resources

B) To track project schedules

C) To identify potential portfolio components

D) To choose the most valuable portfolio components based on strategic alignment

Answer: D) To choose the most valuable portfolio components based on strategic alignment

Explanation: The main purpose of portfolio component selection evaluation is to choose the most valuable portfolio components based on their strategic alignment and potential contribution to the organization's goals.

Question 229:

Which role in portfolio management is responsible for ensuring that portfolio components are executed efficiently and effectively?

A) Project manager

B) Portfolio manager

C) Program manager

D) Chief Operating Officer

Answer: B) Portfolio manager

Explanation: The portfolio manager is responsible for ensuring that portfolio components are executed efficiently and effectively to achieve the organization's strategic goals.

Question 230:

What is the primary goal of portfolio component closure evaluation in portfolio management?

A) To allocate project resources

B) To track project schedules

C) To assess the outcomes and value delivered by portfolio components

D) To identify potential risks to portfolio components

Answer: C) To assess the outcomes and value delivered by portfolio components

Explanation: The primary goal of portfolio component closure evaluation is to assess the outcomes and value delivered by portfolio components, determining their contribution to strategic goals and lessons learned.

Question 231:

In portfolio management, what is the purpose of portfolio component resource allocation management?

A) To execute project tasks

B) To track project schedules

C) To manage project resources effectively

D) To ensure that the right resources are allocated to portfolio components

Answer: D) To ensure that the right resources are allocated to portfolio components

Explanation: The purpose of portfolio component resource allocation management is to ensure that the right resources, including people, budget, and materials, are allocated to portfolio components to achieve strategic objectives efficiently.

Question 232:

What is the main objective of portfolio component governance in portfolio management?

A) To execute project tasks

B) To allocate project resources

C) To ensure that portfolio components are aligned with strategic goals

D) To establish processes for effective decision-making and oversight

Answer: D) To establish processes for effective decision-making and oversight

Explanation: The main objective of portfolio component governance is to establish processes for effective decision-making and oversight to ensure that portfolio components align with strategic goals and are executed successfully.

Question 233:

Which PfMP domain focuses on defining and implementing processes for effective stakeholder engagement and communication within the portfolio?

A) Stakeholder engagement

B) Governance

C) Portfolio performance

D) Resource management

Answer: A) Stakeholder engagement

Explanation: The stakeholder engagement domain focuses on defining and implementing processes for effective stakeholder engagement and communication within the portfolio to ensure their involvement and support.

Question 234:

What is the primary focus of portfolio component risk management in portfolio management?

A) To execute project tasks

B) To allocate project resources

C) To ensure that portfolio components are aligned with strategic goals

D) To identify and mitigate potential risks to portfolio components

Answer: D) To identify and mitigate potential risks to portfolio components

Explanation: The primary focus of portfolio component risk management is to identify and mitigate potential risks to portfolio components, ensuring their alignment with strategic goals and minimizing uncertainties.

Question 235:

Which role in portfolio management is responsible for defining and implementing processes for effective governance and decision-making within the portfolio?

A) Project manager

B) Portfolio manager

C) Governance officer

D) Chief Executive Officer

Answer: C) Governance officer

Explanation: The governance officer is responsible for defining and implementing processes for effective governance and decision-making within the portfolio, ensuring compliance with policies and strategic alignment.

Question 236:

What is the main purpose of portfolio component selection evaluation in portfolio management?

A) To allocate project resources

B) To track project schedules

C) To identify potential portfolio components

D) To choose the most valuable portfolio components based on strategic alignment

Answer: D) To choose the most valuable portfolio components based on strategic alignment

Explanation: The main purpose of portfolio component selection evaluation is to choose the most valuable portfolio components based on their strategic alignment and potential contribution to the organization's goals.

Question 237:

In portfolio management, what is the purpose of portfolio component integration management?

A) To execute project tasks

B) To allocate project resources

C) To manage project schedules

D) To ensure that portfolio components work together cohesively

Answer: D) To ensure that portfolio components work together cohesively

Explanation: Portfolio component integration management aims to ensure that portfolio components work together cohesively to achieve the organization's strategic goals.

Question 238:

What is the main goal of portfolio component governance in portfolio management?

A) To execute project tasks

B) To allocate project resources

C) To ensure that portfolio components are aligned with strategic goals

D) To establish processes for effective decision-making and oversight

Answer: C) To ensure that portfolio components are aligned with strategic goals

Explanation: The main goal of portfolio component governance is to ensure that portfolio components are aligned with strategic goals and are executed successfully according to established guidelines.

Question 239:

Which PfMP domain focuses on defining and implementing processes for effective risk management within the portfolio?

A) Financial management

B) Resource management

C) Governance

D) Risk management

Answer: D) Risk management

Explanation: The risk management domain focuses on defining and implementing processes for effective risk management within the portfolio, identifying and mitigating risks that may impact strategic goals.

Question 240:

What is the primary focus of portfolio component execution management in portfolio management?

A) To allocate project resources

B) To track project schedules

C) To ensure that portfolio components are executed according to established guidelines

D) To identify potential risks to portfolio components

Answer: C) To ensure that portfolio components are executed according to established guidelines

Explanation: Portfolio component execution management focuses on ensuring that portfolio components are executed according to established guidelines and processes, aligning with strategic goals.

Question 241:

What is the primary objective of portfolio component evaluation in portfolio management?

A) To allocate project resources

B) To track project schedules

C) To assess the outcomes and value delivered by portfolio components

D) To identify potential risks to portfolio components

Answer: C) To assess the outcomes and value delivered by portfolio components

Explanation: The primary objective of portfolio component evaluation is to assess the outcomes and value delivered by portfolio components, determining their contribution to strategic goals and lessons learned.

Question 242:

Which PfMP domain focuses on defining and implementing processes for effective governance and decision-making within the portfolio?

A) Stakeholder engagement

B) Governance

C) Portfolio performance

D) Resource management

Answer: B) Governance

Explanation: The governance domain focuses on defining and implementing processes for effective governance and decision-making within the portfolio, ensuring compliance with policies and strategic alignment.

Question 243:

What is the main purpose of portfolio component closure evaluation in portfolio management?

A) To allocate project resources

B) To track project schedules

C) To assess the outcomes and value delivered by portfolio components

D) To identify potential risks to portfolio components

Answer: C) To assess the outcomes and value delivered by portfolio components

Explanation: The main purpose of portfolio component closure evaluation is to assess the outcomes and value delivered by portfolio components, determining their contribution to strategic goals and lessons learned.

Question 244:

Which role in portfolio management is responsible for ensuring that portfolio components are executed efficiently and effectively?

A) Project manager

B) Portfolio manager

C) Program manager

D) Chief Operating Officer

Answer: B) Portfolio manager

Explanation: The portfolio manager is responsible for ensuring that portfolio components are executed efficiently and effectively to achieve the organization's strategic goals.

Question 245:

What is the main focus of portfolio component risk management in portfolio management?

A) To execute project tasks

B) To allocate project resources

C) To ensure that portfolio components are aligned with strategic goals

D) To identify and mitigate potential risks to portfolio components

Answer: D) To identify and mitigate potential risks to portfolio components

Explanation: The main focus of portfolio component risk management is to identify and mitigate potential risks to portfolio components, ensuring their alignment with strategic goals and minimizing uncertainties.

Question 246:

Which PfMP domain focuses on defining and implementing processes for effective change management within the portfolio?

A) Financial management

B) Resource management

C) Governance

D) Change management

Answer: D) Change management

Explanation: The change management domain focuses on defining and implementing processes for effective change management within the portfolio, ensuring successful adoption of changes.

Question 247:

In portfolio management, what is the purpose of portfolio component integration management?

A) To execute project tasks

B) To allocate project resources

C) To manage project schedules

D) To ensure that portfolio components work together cohesively

Answer: D) To ensure that portfolio components work together cohesively

Explanation: Portfolio component integration management aims to ensure that portfolio components work together cohesively to achieve the organization's strategic goals.

Question 248:

What is the primary goal of portfolio component governance in portfolio management?

A) To execute project tasks

B) To allocate project resources

C) To ensure that portfolio components are aligned with strategic goals

D) To establish processes for effective decision-making and oversight

Answer: C) To ensure that portfolio components are aligned with strategic goals

Explanation: The primary goal of portfolio component governance is to ensure that portfolio components are aligned with strategic goals and are executed successfully according to established guidelines.

Question 249:

Which role in portfolio management is responsible for defining and implementing processes for effective stakeholder engagement and communication within the portfolio?

A) Project manager

B) Portfolio manager

C) Stakeholder engagement officer

D) Chief Communication Officer

Answer: B) Portfolio manager

Explanation: The portfolio manager is responsible for defining and implementing processes for effective stakeholder engagement and communication within the portfolio, ensuring their involvement and support.

Question 250:

What is the main objective of portfolio component selection evaluation in portfolio management?

A) To allocate project resources

B) To track project schedules

C) To identify potential portfolio components

D) To choose the most valuable portfolio components based on strategic alignment

Answer: D) To choose the most valuable portfolio components based on strategic alignment

Explanation: The main objective of portfolio component selection evaluation is to choose the most valuable portfolio components based on their strategic alignment and potential contribution to the organization's goals.

Question 251:

In portfolio management, what is the purpose of portfolio component resource allocation management?

A) To execute project tasks

B) To track project schedules

C) To manage project resources effectively

D) To ensure that the right resources are allocated to portfolio components

Answer: D) To ensure that the right resources are allocated to portfolio components

Explanation: The purpose of portfolio component resource allocation management is to ensure that the right resources, including people, budget, and materials, are allocated to portfolio components for successful execution.

Question 252:

Which PfMP domain focuses on defining and implementing processes for effective communication within the portfolio?

A) Stakeholder engagement

B) Governance

C) Communication management

D) Resource management

Answer: C) Communication management

Explanation: The communication management domain focuses on defining and implementing processes for effective communication within the portfolio, ensuring clear and timely exchange of information.

Question 253:

What is the main purpose of portfolio component evaluation in portfolio management?

A) To allocate project resources

B) To track project schedules

C) To assess the outcomes and value delivered by portfolio components

D) To identify potential risks to portfolio components

Answer: C) To assess the outcomes and value delivered by portfolio components

Explanation: The main purpose of portfolio component evaluation is to assess the outcomes and value delivered by portfolio components, determining their contribution to strategic goals and lessons learned.

Question 254:

Which role in portfolio management is responsible for ensuring that portfolio components are executed efficiently and effectively?

A) Project manager

B) Portfolio manager

C) Program manager

D) Chief Operating Officer

Answer: B) Portfolio manager

Explanation: The portfolio manager is responsible for ensuring that portfolio components are executed efficiently and effectively to achieve the organization's strategic goals.

Question 255:

What is the main focus of portfolio component risk management in portfolio management?

A) To execute project tasks

B) To allocate project resources

C) To ensure that portfolio components are aligned with strategic goals

D) To identify and mitigate potential risks to portfolio components

Answer: D) To identify and mitigate potential risks to portfolio components

Explanation: The main focus of portfolio component risk management is to identify and mitigate potential risks to portfolio components, ensuring their alignment with strategic goals and minimizing uncertainties.

Question 256:

Which PfMP domain focuses on defining and implementing processes for effective change management within the portfolio?

A) Financial management

B) Resource management

C) Governance

D) Change management

Answer: D) Change management

Explanation: The change management domain focuses on defining and implementing processes for effective change management within the portfolio, ensuring successful adoption of changes.

Question 257:

In portfolio management, what is the purpose of portfolio component integration management?

A) To execute project tasks

B) To allocate project resources

C) To manage project schedules

D) To ensure that portfolio components work together cohesively

Answer: D) To ensure that portfolio components work together cohesively

Explanation: Portfolio component integration management aims to ensure that portfolio components work together cohesively to achieve the organization's strategic goals.

Question 258:

What is the primary goal of portfolio component governance in portfolio management?

A) To execute project tasks

B) To allocate project resources

C) To ensure that portfolio components are aligned with strategic goals

D) To establish processes for effective decision-making and oversight

Answer: C) To ensure that portfolio components are aligned with strategic goals

Explanation: The primary goal of portfolio component governance is to ensure that portfolio components are aligned with strategic goals and are executed successfully according to established guidelines.

Question 259:

Which role in portfolio management is responsible for defining and implementing processes for effective stakeholder engagement and communication within the portfolio?

A) Project manager

B) Portfolio manager

C) Stakeholder engagement officer

D) Chief Communication Officer

Answer: B) Portfolio manager

Explanation: The portfolio manager is responsible for defining and implementing processes for effective stakeholder engagement and communication within the portfolio, ensuring their involvement and support.

Question 260:

What is the main objective of portfolio component selection evaluation in portfolio management?

A) To allocate project resources

B) To track project schedules

C) To identify potential portfolio components

D) To choose the most valuable portfolio components based on strategic alignment

Answer: D) To choose the most valuable portfolio components based on strategic alignment

Explanation: The main objective of portfolio component selection evaluation is to choose the most valuable portfolio components based on their strategic alignment and potential contribution to the organization's goals.

Question 261:

Which PfMP domain focuses on defining and implementing processes for effective risk management within the portfolio?

A) Governance

B) Risk management

C) Portfolio performance

D) Resource management

Answer: B) Risk management

Explanation: The risk management domain focuses on defining and implementing processes for effective risk management within the portfolio, ensuring potential risks are identified and managed appropriately.

Question 262:

In portfolio management, what is the primary purpose of portfolio component alignment management?

A) To execute project tasks

B) To allocate project resources

C) To ensure that portfolio components are aligned with strategic goals

D) To identify potential risks to portfolio components

Answer: C) To ensure that portfolio components are aligned with strategic goals

Explanation: The primary purpose of portfolio component alignment management is to ensure that portfolio components are aligned with the organization's strategic goals and objectives.

Question 263:

What role is responsible for overseeing the execution of individual projects and ensuring alignment with the overall portfolio strategy?

A) Portfolio manager

B) Project manager

C) Program manager

D) Portfolio steering committee

Answer: B) Project manager

Explanation: The project manager is responsible for overseeing the execution of individual projects and ensuring they align with the overall portfolio strategy.

Question 264:

Which PfMP domain focuses on defining and implementing processes for effective financial management within the portfolio?

A) Governance

B) Financial management

C) Portfolio performance

D) Resource management

Answer: B) Financial management

Explanation: The financial management domain focuses on defining and implementing processes for effective financial management within the portfolio, ensuring resources are allocated and managed efficiently.

Question 265:

What is the main goal of portfolio component risk management in portfolio management?

A) To execute project tasks

B) To allocate project resources

C) To ensure that portfolio components are aligned with strategic goals

D) To identify and mitigate potential risks to portfolio components

Answer: D) To identify and mitigate potential risks to portfolio components

Explanation: The main goal of portfolio component risk management is to identify and mitigate potential risks that may impact the successful execution of portfolio components.

Question 266:

Which PfMP domain focuses on defining and implementing processes for effective resource management within the portfolio?

A) Governance

B) Financial management

C) Portfolio performance

D) Resource management

Answer: D) Resource management

Explanation: The resource management domain focuses on defining and implementing processes for effective resource management within the portfolio, ensuring resources are allocated optimally.

Question 267:

In portfolio management, what is the purpose of portfolio component closure evaluation?

A) To execute project tasks

B) To allocate project resources

C) To assess the outcomes and value delivered by portfolio components

D) To identify potential risks to portfolio components

Answer: C) To assess the outcomes and value delivered by portfolio components

Explanation: The purpose of portfolio component closure evaluation is to assess the outcomes and value delivered by portfolio components, determining their contribution to strategic goals and lessons learned.

Question 268:

What is the primary objective of portfolio component integration management in portfolio management?

A) To execute project tasks

B) To allocate project resources

C) To ensure that portfolio components work together cohesively

D) To identify potential portfolio components

Answer: C) To ensure that portfolio components work together cohesively

Explanation: The primary objective of portfolio component integration management is to ensure that portfolio components work together cohesively to achieve the organization's strategic goals.

Question 269:

In portfolio management, what is the main focus of portfolio component governance?

A) To execute project tasks

B) To allocate project resources

C) To ensure that portfolio components are aligned with strategic goals

D) To establish processes for effective decision-making and oversight

Answer: D) To establish processes for effective decision-making and oversight

Explanation: The main focus of portfolio component governance is to establish processes for effective decision-making and oversight, ensuring that portfolio components are executed successfully and aligned with strategic goals.

Question 270:

Which role in portfolio management is responsible for defining and implementing processes for effective stakeholder engagement and communication within the portfolio?

A) Project manager

B) Portfolio manager

C) Stakeholder engagement officer

D) Chief Communication Officer

Answer: B) Portfolio manager

Explanation: The portfolio manager is responsible for defining and implementing processes for effective stakeholder engagement and communication within the portfolio, ensuring their involvement and support.

Question 271:

What is the primary objective of portfolio component evaluation in portfolio management?

A) To allocate project resources

B) To track project schedules

C) To assess the outcomes and value delivered by portfolio components

D) To identify potential risks to portfolio components

Answer: C) To assess the outcomes and value delivered by portfolio components

Explanation: The primary objective of portfolio component evaluation is to assess the outcomes and value delivered by portfolio components, determining their contribution to strategic goals and lessons learned.

Question 272:

In portfolio management, what is the main focus of portfolio component alignment management?

A) To execute project tasks

B) To allocate project resources

C) To ensure that portfolio components are aligned with strategic goals

D) To identify potential risks to portfolio components

Answer: C) To ensure that portfolio components are aligned with strategic goals

Explanation: The main focus of portfolio component alignment management is to ensure that portfolio components are aligned with the organization's strategic goals and objectives.

Question 273:

Which PfMP domain focuses on defining and implementing processes for effective change management within the portfolio?

A) Governance

B) Financial management

C) Change management

D) Resource management

Answer: C) Change management

Explanation: The change management domain focuses on defining and implementing processes for effective change management within the portfolio, ensuring successful adoption of changes.

Question 274:

What is the main purpose of portfolio component governance in portfolio management?

A) To execute project tasks

B) To allocate project resources

C) To ensure that portfolio components are aligned with strategic goals

D) To establish processes for effective decision-making and oversight

Answer: D) To establish processes for effective decision-making and oversight

Explanation: The main purpose of portfolio component governance is to establish processes for effective decision-making and oversight, ensuring that portfolio components are executed successfully and aligned with strategic goals.

Question 275:

In portfolio management, what is the goal of portfolio component integration management?

A) To execute project tasks

B) To allocate project resources

C) To manage project schedules

D) To ensure that portfolio components work together cohesively

Answer: D) To ensure that portfolio components work together cohesively

Explanation: The goal of portfolio component integration management is to ensure that portfolio components work together cohesively to achieve the organization's strategic goals.

Question 276:

What is the main focus of portfolio component risk management in portfolio management?

A) To execute project tasks

B) To allocate project resources

C) To ensure that portfolio components are aligned with strategic goals

D) To identify and mitigate potential risks to portfolio components

Answer: D) To identify and mitigate potential risks to portfolio components

Explanation: The main focus of portfolio component risk management is to identify and mitigate potential risks to portfolio components, ensuring their alignment with strategic goals and minimizing uncertainties.

Question 277:

Which role in portfolio management is responsible for ensuring that portfolio components are executed efficiently and effectively?

A) Project manager

B) Portfolio manager

C) Program manager

D) Chief Operating Officer

Answer: B) Portfolio manager

Explanation: The portfolio manager is responsible for ensuring that portfolio components are executed efficiently and effectively to achieve the organization's strategic goals.

Question 278:

What is the main goal of portfolio component evaluation in portfolio management?

A) To allocate project resources

B) To track project schedules

C) To assess the outcomes and value delivered by portfolio components

D) To identify potential portfolio components

Answer: C) To assess the outcomes and value delivered by portfolio components

Explanation: The main goal of portfolio component evaluation is to assess the outcomes and value delivered by portfolio components, determining their contribution to strategic goals and lessons learned.

Question 279:

In portfolio management, what is the purpose of portfolio component closure evaluation?

A) To execute project tasks

B) To allocate project resources

C) To assess the outcomes and value delivered by portfolio components

D) To identify potential risks to portfolio components

Answer: C) To assess the outcomes and value delivered by portfolio components

Explanation: The purpose of portfolio component closure evaluation is to assess the outcomes and value delivered by portfolio components, determining their contribution to strategic goals and lessons learned.

Question 280:

Which PfMP domain focuses on defining and implementing processes for effective stakeholder engagement and communication within the portfolio?

A) Stakeholder engagement

B) Governance

C) Communication management

D) Resource management

Answer: C) Communication management

Explanation: The communication management domain focuses on defining and implementing processes for effective stakeholder engagement and communication within the portfolio, ensuring clear and timely exchange of information.

Question 281:

What is the primary objective of portfolio governance in portfolio management?

A) To execute project tasks

B) To allocate project resources

C) To ensure alignment with strategic goals and effective decision-making

D) To identify potential risks to portfolio components

Answer: C) To ensure alignment with strategic goals and effective decision-making

Explanation: The primary objective of portfolio governance is to ensure alignment with strategic goals and effective decision-making, ensuring that portfolio components contribute to the organization's objectives.

Question 282:

Which PfMP domain focuses on defining and implementing processes for effective portfolio risk management?

A) Governance

B) Risk management

C) Portfolio performance

D) Resource management

Answer: B) Risk management

Explanation: The risk management domain focuses on defining and implementing processes for effective portfolio risk management, identifying and managing potential risks to portfolio components.

Question 283:

In portfolio management, what is the main focus of portfolio component closure evaluation?

A) To execute project tasks

B) To allocate project resources

C) To assess the outcomes and value delivered by portfolio components

D) To identify potential risks to portfolio components

Answer: C) To assess the outcomes and value delivered by portfolio components

Explanation: The main focus of portfolio component closure evaluation is to assess the outcomes and value delivered by portfolio components, determining their contribution to strategic goals and lessons learned.

Question 284:

What is the main purpose of portfolio component integration management in portfolio management?

A) To execute project tasks

B) To allocate project resources

C) To ensure that portfolio components work together cohesively

D) To identify potential portfolio components

Answer: C) To ensure that portfolio components work together cohesively

Explanation: The main purpose of portfolio component integration management is to ensure that portfolio components work together cohesively to achieve the organization's strategic goals.

Question 285:

In portfolio management, what role is responsible for ensuring that portfolio components are aligned with strategic goals and objectives?

A) Portfolio manager

B) Project manager

C) Program manager

D) Chief Executive Officer (CEO)

Answer: A) Portfolio manager

Explanation: The portfolio manager is responsible for ensuring that portfolio components are aligned with strategic goals and objectives, guiding their successful execution.

Question 286:

Which PfMP domain focuses on defining and implementing processes for effective portfolio resource management?

A) Governance

B) Financial management

C) Portfolio performance

D) Resource management

Answer: D) Resource management

Explanation: The resource management domain focuses on defining and implementing processes for effective portfolio resource management, ensuring optimal allocation of resources.

Question 287:

What is the main goal of portfolio component risk management in portfolio management?

A) To execute project tasks

B) To allocate project resources

C) To ensure that portfolio components are aligned with strategic goals

D) To identify and mitigate potential risks to portfolio components

Answer: D) To identify and mitigate potential risks to portfolio components

Explanation: The main goal of portfolio component risk management is to identify and mitigate potential risks that may impact the successful execution of portfolio components.

Question 288:

In portfolio management, what is the purpose of portfolio component evaluation?

A) To execute project tasks

B) To allocate project resources

C) To assess the outcomes and value delivered by portfolio components

D) To identify potential risks to portfolio components

Answer: C) To assess the outcomes and value delivered by portfolio components

Explanation: The purpose of portfolio component evaluation is to assess the outcomes and value delivered by portfolio components, determining their contribution to strategic goals and lessons learned.

Question 289:

What is the primary focus of portfolio component alignment management in portfolio management?

A) To execute project tasks

B) To allocate project resources

C) To ensure that portfolio components are aligned with strategic goals

D) To identify potential risks to portfolio components

Answer: C) To ensure that portfolio components are aligned with strategic goals

Explanation: The primary focus of portfolio component alignment management is to ensure that portfolio components are aligned with the organization's strategic goals and objectives.

Question 290:

In portfolio management, what is the role of the portfolio steering committee?

A) To execute project tasks

B) To allocate project resources

C) To ensure that portfolio components are aligned with strategic goals

D) To establish processes for effective decision-making and oversight

Answer: D) To establish processes for effective decision-making and oversight

Explanation: The role of the portfolio steering committee is to establish processes for effective decision-making and oversight, ensuring that portfolio components are executed successfully and aligned with strategic goals.

Question 291:

Which PfMP domain focuses on defining and implementing processes for effective financial management within the portfolio?

A) Governance

B) Financial management

C) Portfolio performance

D) Resource management

Answer: B) Financial management

Explanation: The financial management domain focuses on defining and implementing processes for effective financial management within the portfolio, ensuring optimal allocation of funds.

Question 292:

In portfolio management, what is the primary focus of portfolio component integration management?

A) To execute project tasks

B) To allocate project resources

C) To manage project schedules

D) To ensure that portfolio components work together cohesively

Answer: D) To ensure that portfolio components work together cohesively

Explanation: The primary focus of portfolio component integration management is to ensure that portfolio components work together cohesively to achieve the organization's strategic goals.

Question 293:

What is the main goal of portfolio component evaluation in portfolio management?

A) To allocate project resources

B) To track project schedules

C) To assess the outcomes and value delivered by portfolio components

D) To identify potential portfolio components

Answer: C) To assess the outcomes and value delivered by portfolio components

Explanation: The main goal of portfolio component evaluation is to assess the outcomes and value delivered by portfolio components, determining their contribution to strategic goals and lessons learned.

Question 294:

In portfolio management, what is the purpose of portfolio component closure evaluation?

A) To execute project tasks

B) To allocate project resources

C) To assess the outcomes and value delivered by portfolio components

D) To identify potential risks to portfolio components

Answer: C) To assess the outcomes and value delivered by portfolio components

Explanation: The purpose of portfolio component closure evaluation is to assess the outcomes and value delivered by portfolio components, determining their contribution to strategic goals and lessons learned.

Question 295:

Which role in portfolio management is responsible for ensuring that portfolio components are executed efficiently and effectively?

A) Project manager

B) Portfolio manager

C) Program manager

D) Chief Operating Officer

Answer: B) Portfolio manager

Explanation: The portfolio manager is responsible for ensuring that portfolio components are executed efficiently and effectively to achieve the organization's strategic goals.

Question 296:

What is the main goal of portfolio component risk management in portfolio management?

A) To execute project tasks

B) To allocate project resources

C) To ensure that portfolio components are aligned with strategic goals

D) To identify and mitigate potential risks to portfolio components

Answer: D) To identify and mitigate potential risks to portfolio components

Explanation: The main goal of portfolio component risk management is to identify and mitigate potential risks to portfolio components, ensuring their alignment with strategic goals and minimizing uncertainties.

Question 297:

Which PfMP domain focuses on defining and implementing processes for effective stakeholder engagement and communication within the portfolio?

A) Stakeholder engagement

B) Governance

C) Communication management

D) Resource management

Answer: C) Communication management

Explanation: The communication management domain focuses on defining and implementing processes for effective stakeholder engagement and communication within the portfolio, ensuring clear and timely exchange of information.

Question 298:

What is the main purpose of portfolio component governance in portfolio management?

A) To execute project tasks

B) To allocate project resources

C) To ensure that portfolio components are aligned with strategic goals

D) To establish processes for effective decision-making and oversight

Answer: D) To establish processes for effective decision-making and oversight

Explanation: The main purpose of portfolio component governance is to establish processes for effective decision-making and oversight, ensuring that portfolio components are executed successfully and aligned with strategic goals.

Question 299:

In portfolio management, what is the goal of portfolio component integration management?

A) To execute project tasks

B) To allocate project resources

C) To manage project schedules

D) To ensure that portfolio components work together cohesively

Answer: D) To ensure that portfolio components work together cohesively

Explanation: The goal of portfolio component integration management is to ensure that portfolio components work together cohesively to achieve the organization's strategic goals.

Question 300:

Which PfMP domain focuses on defining and implementing processes for effective portfolio resource management?

A) Governance

B) Financial management

C) Portfolio performance

D) Resource management

Answer: D) Resource management

Explanation: The resource management domain focuses on defining and implementing processes for effective portfolio resource management, ensuring optimal allocation of resources.

Question 301:

What is the primary purpose of portfolio governance in portfolio management?

A) To execute project tasks

B) To allocate project resources

C) To ensure alignment with strategic goals and effective decision-making

D) To identify potential risks to portfolio components

Answer: C) To ensure alignment with strategic goals and effective decision-making

Explanation: The primary purpose of portfolio governance is to ensure alignment with strategic goals and effective decision-making, ensuring that the portfolio components contribute to the organization's objectives.

Question 302:

In portfolio management, what is the role of the portfolio manager regarding portfolio components?

A) To execute project tasks

B) To allocate project resources

C) To ensure alignment with strategic goals

D) To identify potential risks to portfolio components

Answer: C) To ensure alignment with strategic goals

Explanation: The role of the portfolio manager in portfolio management is to ensure alignment of portfolio components with the organization's strategic goals and objectives.

Question 303:

What is the main focus of portfolio component risk management in portfolio management?

A) To execute project tasks

B) To allocate project resources

C) To ensure alignment with strategic goals

D) To identify and mitigate potential risks to portfolio components

Answer: D) To identify and mitigate potential risks to portfolio components

Explanation: The main focus of portfolio component risk management is to identify and mitigate potential risks to portfolio components, ensuring their alignment with strategic goals and minimizing uncertainties.

Question 304:

Which PfMP domain focuses on defining and implementing processes for effective financial management within the portfolio?

A) Governance

B) Financial management

C) Portfolio performance

D) Resource management

Answer: B) Financial management

Explanation: The financial management domain focuses on defining and implementing processes for effective financial management within the portfolio, ensuring optimal allocation of funds.

Question 305:

In portfolio management, what is the primary purpose of portfolio component alignment management?

A) To execute project tasks

B) To allocate project resources

C) To ensure alignment with strategic goals

D) To identify potential risks to portfolio components

Answer: C) To ensure alignment with strategic goals

Explanation: The primary purpose of portfolio component alignment management is to ensure that portfolio components are aligned with the organization's strategic goals and objectives.

Question 306:

Which role is responsible for ensuring that portfolio components are executed efficiently and effectively in portfolio management?

A) Project manager

B) Portfolio manager

C) Program manager

D) Chief Operating Officer

Answer: B) Portfolio manager

Explanation: The portfolio manager is responsible for ensuring that portfolio components are executed efficiently and effectively to achieve the organization's strategic goals.

Question 307:

What is the main goal of portfolio component evaluation in portfolio management?

A) To allocate project resources

B) To track project schedules

C) To assess the outcomes and value delivered by portfolio components

D) To identify potential portfolio components

Answer: C) To assess the outcomes and value delivered by portfolio components

Explanation: The main goal of portfolio component evaluation is to assess the outcomes and value delivered by portfolio components, determining their contribution to strategic goals and lessons learned.

Question 308:

In portfolio management, what is the purpose of portfolio component closure evaluation?

A) To execute project tasks

B) To allocate project resources

C) To assess the outcomes and value delivered by portfolio components

D) To identify potential risks to portfolio components

Answer: C) To assess the outcomes and value delivered by portfolio components

Explanation: The purpose of portfolio component closure evaluation is to assess the outcomes and value delivered by portfolio components, determining their contribution to strategic goals and lessons learned.

Question 309:

What is the main focus of portfolio component integration management in portfolio management?

A) To execute project tasks

B) To allocate project resources

C) To manage project schedules

D) To ensure that portfolio components work together cohesively

Answer: D) To ensure that portfolio components work together cohesively

Explanation: The main focus of portfolio component integration management is to ensure that portfolio components work together cohesively to achieve the organization's strategic goals.

Question 310:

Which PfMP domain focuses on defining and implementing processes for effective stakeholder engagement and communication within the portfolio?

A) Stakeholder engagement

B) Governance

C) Communication management

D) Resource management

Answer: C) Communication management

Explanation: The communication management domain focuses on defining and implementing processes for effective stakeholder engagement and communication within the portfolio, ensuring clear and timely exchange of information.

Question 311:

What is the main purpose of portfolio component governance in portfolio management?

A) To execute project tasks

B) To allocate project resources

C) To ensure that portfolio components are aligned with strategic goals

D) To establish processes for effective decision-making and oversight

Answer: D) To establish processes for effective decision-making and oversight

Explanation: The main purpose of portfolio component governance is to establish processes for effective decision-making and oversight, ensuring that portfolio components are executed successfully and aligned with strategic goals.

Question 312:

In portfolio management, what is the goal of portfolio component integration management?

A) To execute project tasks

B) To allocate project resources

C) To manage project schedules

D) To ensure that portfolio components work together cohesively

Answer: D) To ensure that portfolio components work together cohesively

Explanation: The goal of portfolio component integration management is to ensure that portfolio components work together cohesively to achieve the organization's strategic goals.

Question 313:

Which PfMP domain focuses on defining and implementing processes for effective portfolio resource management?

A) Governance

B) Financial management

C) Portfolio performance

D) Resource management

Answer: D) Resource management

Explanation: The resource management domain focuses on defining and implementing processes for effective portfolio resource management, ensuring optimal allocation of resources.

Question 314:

In portfolio management, what is the goal of portfolio component risk management?

A) To execute project tasks

B) To allocate project resources

C) To ensure alignment with strategic goals

D) To identify and mitigate potential risks to portfolio components

Answer: D) To identify and mitigate potential risks to portfolio components

Explanation: The goal of portfolio component risk management is to identify and mitigate potential risks to portfolio components, ensuring their alignment with strategic goals and minimizing uncertainties.

Question 315:

What is the primary goal of portfolio component alignment management in portfolio management?

A) To execute project tasks

B) To allocate project resources

C) To ensure alignment with strategic goals

D) To identify potential risks to portfolio components

Answer: C) To ensure alignment with strategic goals

Explanation: The primary goal of portfolio component alignment management is to ensure that portfolio components are aligned with the organization's strategic goals and objectives.

Question 316:

Which PfMP domain focuses on defining and implementing processes for effective financial management within the portfolio?

A) Governance

B) Financial management

C) Portfolio performance

D) Resource management

Answer: B) Financial management

Explanation: The financial management domain focuses on defining and implementing processes for effective financial management within the portfolio, ensuring optimal allocation of funds.

Question 317:

What is the main purpose of portfolio component integration management in portfolio management?

A) To execute project tasks

B) To allocate project resources

C) To manage project schedules

D) To ensure that portfolio components work together cohesively

Answer: D) To ensure that portfolio components work together cohesively

Explanation: The main purpose of portfolio component integration management is to ensure that portfolio components work together cohesively to achieve the organization's strategic goals.

Question 318:

In portfolio management, what is the primary focus of portfolio component governance?

A) To execute project tasks

B) To allocate project resources

C) To ensure alignment with strategic goals

D) To establish processes for effective decision-making and oversight

Answer: D) To establish processes for effective decision-making and oversight

Explanation: The primary focus of portfolio component governance is to establish processes for effective decision-making and oversight, ensuring that portfolio components are executed successfully and aligned with strategic goals.

Question 319:

What is the main goal of portfolio component evaluation in portfolio management?

A) To allocate project resources

B) To track project schedules

C) To assess the outcomes and value delivered by portfolio components

D) To identify potential portfolio components

Answer: C) To assess the outcomes and value delivered by portfolio components

Explanation: The main goal of portfolio component evaluation is to assess the outcomes and value delivered by portfolio components, determining their contribution to strategic goals and lessons learned.

Question 320:

In portfolio management, what is the primary focus of portfolio component risk management?

A) To execute project tasks

B) To allocate project resources

C) To ensure alignment with strategic goals

D) To identify and mitigate potential risks to portfolio components

Answer: D) To identify and mitigate potential risks to portfolio components

Explanation: The primary focus of portfolio component risk management is to identify and mitigate potential risks to portfolio components, ensuring their alignment with strategic goals and minimizing uncertainties.

Question 321:

Which PfMP domain focuses on defining and implementing processes for effective portfolio communication management?

A) Stakeholder engagement

B) Governance

C) Communication management

D) Resource management

Answer: C) Communication management

Explanation: The communication management domain focuses on defining and implementing processes for effective portfolio communication management, ensuring clear and timely exchange of information.

Question 322:

What is the primary purpose of portfolio component integration management in portfolio management?

A) To execute project tasks

B) To allocate project resources

C) To manage project schedules

D) To ensure that portfolio components work together cohesively

Answer: D) To ensure that portfolio components work together cohesively

Explanation: The primary purpose of portfolio component integration management is to ensure that portfolio components work together cohesively to achieve the organization's strategic goals.

Question 323:

In portfolio management, what is the main goal of portfolio component evaluation?

A) To allocate project resources

B) To track project schedules

C) To assess the outcomes and value delivered by portfolio components

D) To identify potential portfolio components

Answer: C) To assess the outcomes and value delivered by portfolio components

Explanation: The main goal of portfolio component evaluation is to assess the outcomes and value delivered by portfolio components, determining their contribution to strategic goals and lessons learned.

Question 324:

Which role is responsible for ensuring that portfolio components are executed efficiently and effectively in portfolio management?

A) Project manager

B) Portfolio manager

C) Program manager

D) Chief Operating Officer

Answer: B) Portfolio manager

Explanation: The portfolio manager is responsible for ensuring that portfolio components are executed efficiently and effectively to achieve the organization's strategic goals.

Question 325:

What is the main purpose of portfolio component alignment management in portfolio management?

A) To execute project tasks

B) To allocate project resources

C) To ensure alignment with strategic goals

D) To identify potential risks to portfolio components

Answer: C) To ensure alignment with strategic goals

Explanation: The main purpose of portfolio component alignment management is to ensure that portfolio components are aligned with the organization's strategic goals and objectives.

Question 326:

Which PfMP domain focuses on defining and implementing processes for effective portfolio resource management?

A) Governance

B) Financial management

C) Portfolio performance

D) Resource management

Answer: D) Resource management

Explanation: The resource management domain focuses on defining and implementing processes for effective portfolio resource management, ensuring optimal allocation of resources.

Question 327:

In portfolio management, what is the primary focus of portfolio component governance?

A) To execute project tasks

B) To allocate project resources

C) To ensure alignment with strategic goals

D) To establish processes for effective decision-making and oversight

Answer: D) To establish processes for effective decision-making and oversight

Explanation: The primary focus of portfolio component governance is to establish processes for effective decision-making and oversight, ensuring that portfolio components are executed successfully and aligned with strategic goals.

Question 328:

What is the main goal of portfolio component integration management in portfolio management?

A) To execute project tasks

B) To allocate project resources

C) To manage project schedules

D) To ensure that portfolio components work together cohesively

Answer: D) To ensure that portfolio components work together cohesively

Explanation: The main goal of portfolio component integration management is to ensure that portfolio components work together cohesively to achieve the organization's strategic goals.

Question 329:

In portfolio management, what is the primary purpose of portfolio component risk management?

A) To execute project tasks

B) To allocate project resources

C) To ensure alignment with strategic goals

D) To identify and mitigate potential risks to portfolio components

Answer: D) To identify and mitigate potential risks to portfolio components

Explanation: The primary purpose of portfolio component risk management is to identify and mitigate potential risks to portfolio components, ensuring their alignment with strategic goals and minimizing uncertainties.

Question 330:

Which PfMP domain focuses on defining and implementing processes for effective portfolio communication management?

A) Stakeholder engagement

B) Governance

C) Communication management

D) Resource management

Answer: C) Communication management

Explanation: The communication management domain focuses on defining and implementing processes for effective portfolio communication management, ensuring clear and timely exchange of information.

Question 331:

What is the primary purpose of portfolio component integration management in portfolio management?

A) To execute project tasks

B) To allocate project resources

C) To manage project schedules

D) To ensure that portfolio components work together cohesively

Answer: D) To ensure that portfolio components work together cohesively

Explanation: The primary purpose of portfolio component integration management is to ensure that portfolio components work together cohesively to achieve the organization's strategic goals.

Question 332:

In portfolio management, what is the main goal of portfolio component evaluation?

A) To allocate project resources

B) To track project schedules

C) To assess the outcomes and value delivered by portfolio components

D) To identify potential portfolio components

Answer: C) To assess the outcomes and value delivered by portfolio components

Explanation: The main goal of portfolio component evaluation is to assess the outcomes and value delivered by portfolio components, determining their contribution to strategic goals and lessons learned.

Question 333:

Which role is responsible for ensuring that portfolio components are executed efficiently and effectively in portfolio management?

A) Project manager

B) Portfolio manager

C) Program manager

D) Chief Operating Officer

Answer: B) Portfolio manager

Explanation: The portfolio manager is responsible for ensuring that portfolio components are executed efficiently and effectively to achieve the organization's strategic goals.

Question 334:

What is the main purpose of portfolio component alignment management in portfolio management?

A) To execute project tasks

B) To allocate project resources

C) To ensure alignment with strategic goals

D) To identify potential risks to portfolio components

Answer: C) To ensure alignment with strategic goals

Explanation: The main purpose of portfolio component alignment management is to ensure that portfolio components are aligned with the organization's strategic goals and objectives.

Question 335:

Which PfMP domain focuses on defining and implementing processes for effective portfolio resource management?

A) Governance

B) Financial management

C) Portfolio performance

D) Resource management

Answer: D) Resource management

Explanation: The resource management domain focuses on defining and implementing processes for effective portfolio resource management, ensuring optimal allocation of resources.

Question 336:

In portfolio management, what is the primary focus of portfolio component governance?

A) To execute project tasks

B) To allocate project resources

C) To ensure alignment with strategic goals

D) To establish processes for effective decision-making and oversight

Answer: D) To establish processes for effective decision-making and oversight

Explanation: The primary focus of portfolio component governance is to establish processes for effective decision-making and oversight, ensuring that portfolio components are executed successfully and aligned with strategic goals.

Question 337:

What is the main goal of portfolio component integration management in portfolio management?

A) To execute project tasks

B) To allocate project resources

C) To manage project schedules

D) To ensure that portfolio components work together cohesively

Answer: D) To ensure that portfolio components work together cohesively

Explanation: The main goal of portfolio component integration management is to ensure that portfolio components work together cohesively to achieve the organization's strategic goals.

Question 338:

In portfolio management, what is the primary purpose of portfolio component risk management?

A) To execute project tasks

B) To allocate project resources

C) To ensure alignment with strategic goals

D) To identify and mitigate potential risks to portfolio components

Answer: D) To identify and mitigate potential risks to portfolio components

Explanation: The primary purpose of portfolio component risk management is to identify and mitigate potential risks to portfolio components, ensuring their alignment with strategic goals and minimizing uncertainties.

Question 339:

Which PfMP domain focuses on defining and implementing processes for effective portfolio communication management?

A) Stakeholder engagement

B) Governance

C) Communication management

D) Resource management

Answer: C) Communication management

Explanation: The communication management domain focuses on defining and implementing processes for effective portfolio communication management, ensuring clear and timely exchange of information.

Question 340:

What is the primary purpose of portfolio component integration management in portfolio management?

A) To execute project tasks

B) To allocate project resources

C) To manage project schedules

D) To ensure that portfolio components work together cohesively

Answer: D) To ensure that portfolio components work together cohesively

Explanation: The primary purpose of portfolio component integration management is to ensure that portfolio components work together cohesively to achieve the organization's strategic goals.

Additional TRICKY Q&A

Question 1:

Which of the following terms refers to the process of systematically evaluating and selecting portfolio components based on their alignment with the organization's strategic objectives?

A) Benefit Realization

B) Portfolio Analysis

C) Resource Allocation

D) Risk Management

Explanation:

The correct answer is B) Portfolio Analysis. Portfolio analysis involves evaluating and selecting portfolio components based on their alignment with strategic objectives and their potential benefits.

Question 2:

In a portfolio context, which technique involves evaluating and comparing various portfolio scenarios to determine their potential impact on achieving strategic objectives?

A) Sensitivity Analysis

B) Monte Carlo Simulation

C) Scenario Analysis

D) Cost-Benefit Analysis

Explanation:

The correct answer is C) Scenario Analysis. Scenario analysis involves evaluating different portfolio scenarios to assess their potential impact on strategic objectives, helping decision-makers make informed choices.

Question 3:

Which component of the PfMP framework emphasizes assessing the overall health and performance of the portfolio and identifying areas for improvement?

A) Portfolio Risk Management

B) Portfolio Governance Management

C) Portfolio Strategic Management

D) Portfolio Performance Management

Explanation:

The correct answer is D) Portfolio Performance Management. This component focuses on monitoring and assessing portfolio health, performance, and alignment with strategic goals.

Question 4:

Which type of dependency exists between portfolio components that are mutually exclusive and only one can be selected for implementation?

A) Finish-to-Start

B) Start-to-Start

C) Mandatory

D) Discretionary

Explanation:

The correct answer is C) Mandatory. Mandatory dependencies represent situations where one portfolio component must be selected over another due to exclusivity.

Question 5:

During which phase of the portfolio management lifecycle are portfolio components selected and aligned with strategic objectives?

A) Portfolio Definition

B) Portfolio Planning

C) Portfolio Execution

D) Portfolio Monitoring and Control

Explanation:

The correct answer is B) Portfolio Planning. This phase involves selecting and aligning portfolio components with strategic objectives before moving into execution.

Question 6:

Which technique helps identify potential risks and uncertainties in a portfolio by considering a wide range of scenarios and their impact on strategic goals?

A) Monte Carlo Simulation

B) SWOT Analysis

C) Earned Value Analysis

D) Sensitivity Analysis

Explanation:

The correct answer is A) Monte Carlo Simulation. Monte Carlo Simulation is a powerful technique for assessing risks and uncertainties by simulating various scenarios and their potential impact on portfolio outcomes.

Question 7:

In a portfolio context, what term refers to the total financial value of an investment or project over its entire lifecycle?

A) Net Present Value (NPV)

B) Internal Rate of Return (IRR)

C) Return on Investment (ROI)

D) Whole Life Cost

Explanation:

The correct answer is D) Whole Life Cost. This term refers to the overall financial value of an investment or project throughout its lifecycle, encompassing various costs and benefits.

Question 8:

During which phase of the portfolio management lifecycle is the portfolio strategy refined and detailed planning activities take place?

A) Portfolio Definition

B) Portfolio Planning

C) Portfolio Execution

D) Portfolio Monitoring and Control

Explanation:

The correct answer is B) Portfolio Planning. This phase involves refining the portfolio strategy and conducting detailed planning activities to ensure successful execution.

Question 9:

Which portfolio management technique involves categorizing portfolio components based on their risk and return profiles to create a balanced portfolio?

A) Benefit Realization

B) Portfolio Prioritization

C) Portfolio Balancing

D) Portfolio Optimization

Explanation:

The correct answer is C) Portfolio Balancing. This technique aims to create a balanced portfolio by categorizing components based on risk and return considerations.

Question 10:

What term refers to the set of interconnected and interdependent programs, projects, and operational activities that are managed and coordinated as a whole to achieve strategic objectives?

A) Portfolio

B) Program

C) Project

D) Initiative

Explanation:

The correct answer is A) Portfolio. A portfolio consists of various programs, projects, and operational activities that are managed collectively to achieve strategic objectives.

Question 11:

Which type of dependency exists between portfolio components that can be influenced by the portfolio manager's discretion?

A) Finish-to-Start

B) Start-to-Start

C) Mandatory

D) Discretionary

Explanation:

The correct answer is D) Discretionary. Discretionary dependencies represent situations where the portfolio manager can use their judgment to decide on the sequence of components.

Question 12:

During the portfolio management lifecycle, which phase involves aligning portfolio components with the organization's strategic objectives?

A) Portfolio Definition

B) Portfolio Planning

C) Portfolio Execution

D) Portfolio Monitoring and Control

Explanation:

The correct answer is B) Portfolio Planning. This phase focuses on selecting and aligning portfolio components with strategic objectives.

Question 13:

What type of risk is associated with the uncertainty of achieving strategic objectives due to external factors beyond the organization's control?

A) Strategic Risk

B) Operational Risk

C) Financial Risk

D) Schedule Risk

Explanation:

The correct answer is A) Strategic Risk. Strategic risks pertain to uncertainties related to achieving strategic objectives, often influenced by external factors.

Question 14:

Which technique helps determine the feasibility of implementing portfolio components by considering constraints such as resource availability and budget limitations?

A) SWOT Analysis

B) Cost-Benefit Analysis

C) Resource Optimization

D) Feasibility Study

Explanation:

The correct answer is D) Feasibility Study. A feasibility study assesses the practicality and viability of implementing portfolio components within constraints.

Question 15:

In portfolio management, what term refers to the process of comparing and prioritizing potential portfolio components?

A) Portfolio Balancing

B) Portfolio Optimization

C) Portfolio Prioritization

D) Portfolio Selection

Explanation:

The correct answer is C) Portfolio Prioritization. This process involves comparing and ranking potential portfolio components based on predefined criteria.

Question 16:

What technique involves calculating the present value of expected future cash flows to determine the financial attractiveness of an investment or project?

A) Net Present Value (NPV)

B) Internal Rate of Return (IRR)

C) Payback Period

D) Cost-Benefit Analysis

Explanation:

The correct answer is A) Net Present Value (NPV). NPV calculates the present value of expected future cash flows to assess the financial viability of an investment.

Question 17:

During which phase of the portfolio management lifecycle are actual portfolio performance and progress tracked against the plan?

A) Portfolio Definition

B) Portfolio Planning

C) Portfolio Execution

D) Portfolio Monitoring and Control

Explanation:

The correct answer is D) Portfolio Monitoring and Control. This phase involves tracking and measuring actual portfolio performance against the plan.

Question 18:

Which type of risk is associated with uncertainties in the availability of resources, potential delays, or unexpected events affecting the execution of portfolio components?

A) Strategic Risk

B) Operational Risk

C) Schedule Risk

D) Financial Risk

Explanation:

The correct answer is C) Schedule Risk. Schedule risk pertains to uncertainties that may cause delays or disruptions in the execution of portfolio components.

Question 19:

In a portfolio context, what technique involves evaluating portfolio components based on their contribution to strategic objectives, risks, benefits, and resource requirements?

A) Monte Carlo Simulation

B) Sensitivity Analysis

C) Cost-Benefit Analysis

D) Portfolio Prioritization

Explanation:

The correct answer is D) Portfolio Prioritization. This technique assesses components based on their alignment with strategic objectives, risks, benefits, and resource needs.

Question 20:

During the portfolio management lifecycle, which phase involves implementing the portfolio strategy and executing the portfolio components?

A) Portfolio Definition

B) Portfolio Planning

C) Portfolio Execution

D) Portfolio Monitoring and Control

Explanation:

The correct answer is C) Portfolio Execution. This phase involves carrying out the portfolio strategy by executing the selected components.

Question 21:

What term refers to the process of evaluating portfolio components to ensure they align with the organization's strategic goals and objectives?

A) Portfolio Balancing

B) Portfolio Optimization

C) Portfolio Analysis

D) Portfolio Evaluation

Explanation:

The correct answer is C) Portfolio Analysis. Portfolio analysis involves assessing portfolio components to ensure their alignment with strategic goals and objectives.

Question 22:

Which component of the PfMP framework focuses on defining and managing the roles, responsibilities, and decision-making authority within a portfolio management structure?

A) Portfolio Risk Management

B) Portfolio Governance Management

C) Portfolio Strategic Management

D) Portfolio Performance Management

Explanation:

The correct answer is B) Portfolio Governance Management. This component emphasizes defining roles, responsibilities, and decision-making authority within the portfolio management structure.

Question 23:

In portfolio management, what term refers to the process of assessing the potential impact of external events on portfolio components and their outcomes?

A) Risk Assessment

B) Environmental Analysis

C) Scenario Planning

D) Sensitivity Analysis

Explanation:

The correct answer is B) Environmental Analysis. Environmental analysis involves evaluating the potential impact of external events on portfolio components and their outcomes.

Question 24:

What technique involves comparing portfolio components against predetermined criteria to identify which ones should be included in the portfolio?

A) Feasibility Study

B) Benefit Realization

C) Portfolio Prioritization

D) Portfolio Selection

Explanation:

The correct answer is D) Portfolio Selection. Portfolio selection involves comparing and choosing components based on predefined criteria.

Question 25:

Which type of risk is associated with the potential loss of intellectual property, proprietary information, or competitive advantage?

A) Operational Risk

B) Reputational Risk

C) Intellectual Property Risk

D) Strategic Risk

Explanation:

The correct answer is C) Intellectual Property Risk. This type of risk involves the potential loss of intellectual property, proprietary information, or competitive advantage.

Question 26:

During which phase of the portfolio management lifecycle are potential portfolio components identified and evaluated?

A) Portfolio Definition

B) Portfolio Planning

C) Portfolio Execution

D) Portfolio Monitoring and Control

Explanation:

The correct answer is A) Portfolio Definition. This phase involves identifying and evaluating potential portfolio components.

Question 27:

What technique involves assessing the strengths, weaknesses, opportunities, and threats associated with portfolio components and their impact on achieving strategic objectives?

A) SWOT Analysis

B) Portfolio Analysis

C) Scenario Analysis

D) Cost-Benefit Analysis

Explanation:

The correct answer is A) SWOT Analysis. SWOT analysis evaluates the strengths, weaknesses, opportunities, and threats of portfolio components in relation to strategic objectives.

Question 28:

In portfolio management, what term refers to the process of monitoring and controlling portfolio components to ensure alignment with strategic goals?

A) Portfolio Balancing

B) Portfolio Governance

C) Portfolio Monitoring

D) Portfolio Performance

Explanation:

The correct answer is C) Portfolio Monitoring. Portfolio monitoring involves overseeing and controlling components to ensure they remain aligned with strategic goals.

Question 29:

Which technique involves calculating the expected monetary value of different portfolio scenarios to assess their potential benefits?

A) Decision Tree Analysis

B) Earned Value Analysis

C) Pareto Analysis

D) Risk Analysis

Explanation:

The correct answer is A) Decision Tree Analysis. Decision tree analysis calculates the expected monetary value of various portfolio scenarios to evaluate their benefits.

Question 30:

During the portfolio management lifecycle, which phase involves allocating resources and funding to portfolio components?

A) Portfolio Definition

B) Portfolio Planning

C) Portfolio Execution

D) Portfolio Monitoring and Control

Explanation:

The correct answer is B) Portfolio Planning. This phase involves allocating resources and funding to portfolio components based on their strategic importance.

Question 31:

What type of dependency exists between portfolio components that can occur simultaneously and do not affect the order of execution?

A) Finish-to-Start

B) Start-to-Start

C) Mandatory

D) Discretionary

Explanation:

The correct answer is B) Start-to-Start. Start-to-start dependencies indicate that two components can begin simultaneously without affecting their execution order.

Question 32:

Which type of risk is associated with changes in market conditions, economic factors, or technological advancements impacting portfolio outcomes?

A) Strategic Risk

B) External Risk

C) Environmental Risk

D) Operational Risk

Explanation:

The correct answer is B) External Risk. External risks are influenced by factors outside the organization, such as market changes, economic conditions, or technological advancements.

Question 33:

In a portfolio context, what technique involves calculating the time required for a portfolio component to start generating benefits that offset its costs?

A) Payback Period

B) Return on Investment (ROI)

C) Net Present Value (NPV)

D) Internal Rate of Return (IRR)

Explanation:

The correct answer is A) Payback Period. The payback period calculates the time it takes for the benefits of a component to cover its initial costs.

Question 33:

In a portfolio context, what technique involves calculating the time required for a portfolio component to start generating benefits that offset its costs?

A) Payback Period

B) Return on Investment (ROI)

C) Net Present Value (NPV)

D) Internal Rate of Return (IRR)

Explanation:

The correct answer is A) Payback Period. The payback period calculates the time it takes for the benefits of a component to cover its initial costs.

Question 34:

During the portfolio management lifecycle, which phase involves implementing corrective actions, adjustments, and changes to improve portfolio performance?

A) Portfolio Definition

B) Portfolio Planning

C) Portfolio Execution

D) Portfolio Monitoring and Control

Explanation:

The correct answer is D) Portfolio Monitoring and Control. This phase focuses on implementing corrective actions and changes to enhance portfolio performance.

Question 35:

What term refers to a set of interconnected and aligned projects and programs that help an organization achieve strategic objectives?

A) Portfolio

B) Program

C) Project

D) Initiative

Explanation:

The correct answer is A) Portfolio. A portfolio comprises a collection of interconnected projects and programs that collectively contribute to strategic objectives.

Question 36:

In portfolio management, what term refers to the process of assessing and adjusting the portfolio to accommodate changes in the organization's strategic direction?

A) Portfolio Balancing

B) Portfolio Optimization

C) Portfolio Rebalancing

D) Portfolio Realignment

Explanation:

The correct answer is C) Portfolio Rebalancing. This process involves assessing and adjusting the portfolio to align with changes in the organization's strategic direction.

Question 37:

Which component of the PfMP framework focuses on tracking and measuring the actual performance of portfolio components against defined targets?

A) Portfolio Risk Management

B) Portfolio Governance Management

C) Portfolio Strategic Management

D) Portfolio Performance Management

Explanation:

The correct answer is D) Portfolio Performance Management. This component involves monitoring and measuring the actual performance of portfolio components.

Question 38:

What technique involves estimating the impact of a potential risk event on a portfolio and calculating the expected monetary loss?

A) Decision Tree Analysis

B) Monte Carlo Simulation

C) Sensitivity Analysis

D) SWOT Analysis

Explanation:

The correct answer is B) Monte Carlo Simulation. Monte Carlo simulation estimates the impact of risk events by calculating the expected monetary loss in various scenarios.

Question 39:

During the portfolio management lifecycle, which phase involves defining the portfolio's strategic objectives and establishing its overall direction?

A) Portfolio Definition

B) Portfolio Planning

C) Portfolio Execution

D) Portfolio Monitoring and Control

Explanation:

The correct answer is A) Portfolio Definition. This phase involves defining the strategic objectives and overall direction of the portfolio.

Question 40:

In portfolio management, what term refers to the process of selecting and implementing portfolio components to achieve strategic goals?

A) Portfolio Balancing

B) Portfolio Optimization

C) Portfolio Execution

D) Portfolio Monitoring and Control

Explanation:

The correct answer is C) Portfolio Execution. This process involves selecting and implementing portfolio components to accomplish strategic goals.

Question 41:

What term describes the process of assessing portfolio components to ensure they align with the organization's strategic goals and maximize overall value?

A) Portfolio Prioritization

B) Portfolio Optimization

C) Portfolio Alignment

D) Portfolio Balancing

Explanation:

The correct answer is C) Portfolio Alignment. Portfolio alignment involves assessing components to ensure they are in line with strategic goals and maximize value.

Question 42:

Which type of portfolio management focuses on optimizing individual portfolio components to achieve their objectives?

A) Strategic Portfolio Management

B) Tactical Portfolio Management

C) Operational Portfolio Management

D) Project Portfolio Management

Explanation:

The correct answer is B) Tactical Portfolio Management. Tactical portfolio management emphasizes optimizing individual components to achieve their goals.

Question 43:

In portfolio management, what term refers to the process of evaluating and selecting potential portfolio components based on their alignment with strategic goals?

A) Portfolio Optimization

B) Portfolio Balancing

C) Portfolio Selection

D) Portfolio Analysis

Explanation:

The correct answer is D) Portfolio Analysis. Portfolio analysis involves evaluating and selecting components based on their alignment with strategic goals.

Question 44:

Which component of the PfMP framework involves defining the overall vision, goals, and strategy of the portfolio?

A) Portfolio Governance Management

B) Portfolio Strategic Management

C) Portfolio Risk Management

D) Portfolio Performance Management

Explanation:

The correct answer is B) Portfolio Strategic Management. This component focuses on defining the overall vision, goals, and strategy of the portfolio.

Question 45:

What technique involves assessing the potential impact of a risk event on the portfolio's objectives and outcomes?

A) Risk Mitigation

B) Impact Analysis

C) Risk Response Planning

D) Risk Assessment

Explanation:

The correct answer is B) Impact Analysis. Impact analysis assesses the potential effects of a risk event on the portfolio's objectives and outcomes.

Question 46:

During the portfolio management lifecycle, which phase involves establishing governance structures and decision-making processes for the portfolio?

A) Portfolio Definition

B) Portfolio Planning

C) Portfolio Execution

D) Portfolio Monitoring and Control

Explanation:

The correct answer is A) Portfolio Definition. This phase establishes governance structures and decision-making processes for the portfolio.

Question 47:

Which type of dependency between portfolio components indicates that one component must finish before another can start?

A) Finish-to-Start

B) Start-to-Start

C) Finish-to-Finish

D) Start-to-Finish

Explanation:

The correct answer is A) Finish-to-Start. A finish-to-start dependency means one component must finish before another can start.

Question 48:

What technique involves estimating the potential impact of a risk event on the portfolio's financial and non-financial goals?

A) SWOT Analysis

B) Risk Assessment

C) Monte Carlo Simulation

D) Sensitivity Analysis

Explanation:

The correct answer is C) Monte Carlo Simulation. Monte Carlo simulation estimates the impact of risk events on financial and non-financial goals.

Question 49:

In portfolio management, what term refers to the process of reallocating resources and funds among portfolio components to optimize outcomes?

A) Portfolio Optimization

B) Portfolio Balancing

C) Portfolio Adjustment

D) Portfolio Reallocations

Explanation:

The correct answer is B) Portfolio Balancing. Portfolio balancing involves reallocating resources and funds among components to optimize outcomes.

Question 50:

Which component of the PfMP framework focuses on monitoring and evaluating the performance of portfolio components?

A) Portfolio Governance Management

B) Portfolio Strategic Management

C) Portfolio Risk Management

D) Portfolio Performance Management

Explanation:

The correct answer is D) Portfolio Performance Management. This component focuses on monitoring and evaluating the performance of components.

Question 51:

What technique involves analyzing the likelihood and potential impact of portfolio risks to prioritize their management?

A) Risk Assessment

B) Risk Mitigation

C) Risk Probability Analysis

D) Risk Impact Analysis

Explanation:

The correct answer is A) Risk Assessment. Risk assessment analyzes the likelihood and impact of risks to prioritize their management.

Question 52:

In portfolio management, what term refers to the process of integrating new portfolio components and adjusting the portfolio's strategic direction?

A) Portfolio Optimization

B) Portfolio Integration

C) Portfolio Realignment

D) Portfolio Adjustment

Explanation:

The correct answer is B) Portfolio Integration. Portfolio integration involves incorporating new components and adjusting the strategic direction.

Question 53:

During the portfolio management lifecycle, which phase involves aligning portfolio components with the organization's strategic objectives?

A) Portfolio Definition

B) Portfolio Planning

C) Portfolio Execution

D) Portfolio Monitoring and Control

Explanation:

The correct answer is B) Portfolio Planning. This phase aligns portfolio components with the organization's strategic objectives.

Question 54:

Which technique involves analyzing the potential impact of external factors, market trends, and industry changes on portfolio components?

A) SWOT Analysis

B) Environmental Analysis

C) Scenario Planning

D) Sensitivity Analysis

Explanation:

The correct answer is B) Environmental Analysis. Environmental analysis assesses external factors' impact on portfolio components.

Question 55:

What technique involves assessing portfolio components' potential risks and impacts on each other to minimize negative effects?

A) Risk Response Planning

B) Dependency Analysis

C) Monte Carlo Simulation

D) Sensitivity Analysis

Explanation:

The correct answer is B) Dependency Analysis. Dependency analysis evaluates risks and impacts among components to minimize negative effects.

Question 56:

In portfolio management, what term refers to the process of evaluating and adjusting the portfolio's composition to optimize outcomes?

A) Portfolio Optimization

B) Portfolio Balancing

C) Portfolio Adjustment

D) Portfolio Alignment

Explanation:

The correct answer is A) Portfolio Optimization. Portfolio optimization involves evaluating and adjusting composition for optimal outcomes.

Question 57:

Which component of the PfMP framework focuses on ensuring effective communication, decision-making, and accountability in the portfolio?

A) Portfolio Governance Management

B) Portfolio Strategic Management

C) Portfolio Risk Management

D) Portfolio Performance Management

Explanation:

The correct answer is A) Portfolio Governance Management. This component emphasizes effective communication, decision-making, and accountability.

Question 58:

What technique involves evaluating the potential impact of changes in portfolio components on the overall portfolio?

A) Scenario Planning

B) Sensitivity Analysis

C) Risk Assessment

D) SWOT Analysis

Explanation:

The correct answer is B) Sensitivity Analysis. Sensitivity analysis assesses the impact of changes on the portfolio's overall performance.

Question 59:

During the portfolio management lifecycle, which phase involves selecting and prioritizing potential portfolio components?

A) Portfolio Definition

B) Portfolio Planning

C) Portfolio Execution

D) Portfolio Monitoring and Control

Explanation:

The correct answer is B) Portfolio Planning. This phase selects and prioritizes potential components based on strategic goals.

Question 60:

Which type of dependency between portfolio components indicates that they must occur at the same time or in parallel?

A) Start-to-Start

B) Finish-to-Finish

C) Start-to-Finish

D) Finish-to-Start

Explanation:

The correct answer is B) Finish-to-Finish. Finish-to-finish dependencies indicate components occurring at the same time or in parallel.

END NOTE

Congratulations on completing the journey through the "PfMP Exam Companion: Q&A with Explanations." We hope this resource has been invaluable in your preparation for the Portfolio Management Professional (PfMP) exam. Our aim was to provide you with a comprehensive and detailed set of questions and explanations to enhance your understanding of portfolio management concepts and boost your exam confidence.

Remember, earning the PfMP certification is a significant achievement that reflects your expertise and dedication in the field of portfolio management. As you move forward in your career, we encourage you to apply the knowledge gained from this companion to real-world scenarios, further enhancing your ability to lead successful portfolio management initiatives.

Thank you for entrusting us with your exam preparation. We wish you all the best as you embark on this new phase of your professional journey.

**Please note that the example questions provided are for illustrative purposes only and may not reflect the actual questions found in the PMI-PfMP exam. The purpose is to give you an idea of the question format and provide practice in applying your knowledge. It's important to refer to the official PMI resources and study materials to prepare thoroughly for the exam.

**We apologize for any inadvertent repetition of questions in this material. Please rest assured that any instances of repeated questions were not intentional. If you come across any such occurrences, kindly excuse us, and we appreciate your understanding. Our aim is to provide you with comprehensive and unique content to enhance your learning experience and we're here to support you.

Don't miss out!

Visit the website below and you can sign up to receive emails whenever SUJAN publishes a new book. There's no charge and no obligation.

https://books2read.com/r/B-A-JPZY-WQYMC

BOOKS2READ

Connecting independent readers to independent writers.

Also by SUJAN

PMP Practice Test Navigator: Nailing the Exam
PMP Success: Ultimate Exam Questions & Answers
PMP Exam Companion
CAPM Success Blueprint
AgileQuest: Unlocking PMI-ACP Success
PMI-RMP Exam Companion
PMI-PBA Exam Success :A Practical Guide to Ace Business Analysis Questions
CAPM Success Path : MCQs and Explanations for Prep Excellence
CAPM Q-Connect
CAPM Exam Insights: Q&A with Explanations
PMI-ACP Success Path: Q&A with Explanations
PMI-ACP Exam Insights: Q&A with Explanations
PMI-PgMP Exam Insights: Q&A with Explanations
PMI-SP Success Blueprint: Q&A with Explanations
PMI-RMP Success Blueprint :Q&A with Explanations
PfMP Exam Companion: Q&A with Explanations